MAKING WORK
Self-Created Jobs in
Participatory Organizations

ENVIRONMENT, DEVELOPMENT, AND PUBLIC POLICY

A series of volumes under the general editorship of
Lawrence Susskind, *Massachusetts Institute of Technoloy,*
Cambridge, Massachusetts

CITIES AND DEVELOPMENT

Series Editor: Lloyd Rodwin, *Massachusetts Institute of Technology*
Cambridge, Massachusetts

CITIES AND CITY PLANNING
Lloyd Rodwin

THINKING ABOUT DEVELOPMENT
Lisa Peattie

CONSERVING AMERICA'S NEIGHBORHOODS
Robert K. Yin

MAKING WORK
Self-Created Jobs in Participatory Organizations
William Ronco and Lisa Peattie

In preparation

CITIES OF THE MIND
Images and Themes of the City in the Social Sciences
Robert M. Hollister and Lloyd Rodwin

Other subseries:

ENVIRONMENTAL POLICY AND PLANNING
Series Editor: Lawrence Susskind, *Massachusetts Institute of Technology,*
Cambridge, Massachusetts

PUBLIC POLICY AND SOCIAL SERVICES
Series Editor: Gary Marx, *Massachusetts Institute of Technology,*
Cambridge, Massachusetts

MAKING WORK
Self-Created Jobs in Participatory Organizations

WILLIAM RONCO
Northeastern University
Boston, Massachusetts

AND

LISA PEATTIE
Massachusetts Institute of Technology
Cambridge, Massachusetts

WITH
RUSS TANNER, JOAN WOFFORD,
PETER LINKOW, AND SHARON MORIEARTY

PLENUM PRESS • NEW YORK AND LONDON

Library of Congress Cataloging in Publication Data

Ronco, William C.

Making work.
(Environment, development, and public policy. Cities and development)
Bibliography: p.
Includes index.
1. Work—Social aspects. 2. Job satisfaction. 3. Work groups. I. Peattie, Lisa Redfield. II.
Tanner, Russ. III. Title. IV. Series.
HD6955.R66 1983   758.3'128   83-9527
ISBN 0-306-41230-6

©1983 Plenum Press, New York
A Division of Plenum Publishing Corporation
233 Spring Street, New York, N.Y. 10013

Printed in the United States of America

PREFACE

This book began as an exploration of collaborative work organizations. We knew about people in various occupations who had gotten together to form organizations of equals to manage the settings within which they did their work. Among these organizations were a teacher-controlled public school, a fishermen's cooperative, a potters' studio, a public-interest advocacy group, and an architectural firm. We wondered how these groups functioned, and whether and how they contributed to making work satisfying for the individuals in them.

These groups were, of course, pretty small potatoes, but it seemed to us that they provided a way to an understanding of some much larger current issues. Worker satisfaction has surfaced as an issue of current concern and has been represented in research documenting the growing expectations that the members of our society have of their work experience. More workers are more educated now than ever before, and more and more people seem to look to work as a personal outlet, rather than just a source of income.

We saw our small, egalitarian work organizations as providing settings in which people were especially likely to find work satisfying. We wanted to know both the organizational conditions for satisfying work and the conditions under which collaborative work organizations could keep functioning. Since the sociological literature on work satisfaction tends to revolve around issues of autonomy and control, we sought out settings in which workers had maximized autonomy and control.

We knew, of course, that these settings were, by the very attributes for which we had selected them, far from the ordinary job setting. But, we reasoned, if the idea is to make ordinary work more satisfying, we should be looking more closely at settings in which satisfying work is most likely to occur.

Our "subject" organizations are much less constrained than the team approaches and job redesign schemes that have been instituted in a wide variety of applications to encourage worker satisfaction; however, just because we thought the examples represent "extremes," we thought they might provide insights into the more constrained experiments. In addition, we have long been interested in small, participatory organizations *per se* as an important alternative to the evolving, large bureaucratic organization of work.

Part of our study, then, was a study of *organizations*. In his Ph.D. dissertation for the M.I.T. Department of Urban Studies and Planning and the M.I.T. Division for Research and Education, William Ronco studied the five groups as organizations. He focused in particular on three aspects of the organizations' experience:

1. The extent to which the organizations contribute to members' work experience
2. Members' ability to control and govern the organizations
3. The organizations' effectiveness and ability to learn

Some of Ronco's findings are reported and developed in Chapter 8 of this book. (Copies of the dissertation itself are available through the M.I.T. libraries.)

But, in the course of doing the study, a theme emerged that we had not foreseen when we began. This was the problematic character of the category *work* itself.

We had set out to study satisfying work. But work that is satisfying to the worker is not obviously essentially different from any other activity that a person may choose to perform—those activities we call *hobby*, or *amateur performance*, or *volunteering*. Of course, work is usually distinguished from all these by being paid for, but this seemed to us a distinction rather external to the activity itself—and besides, some of the members of the potters' collective really earned their living in ways other than potting.

So we came to examine the way in which the people whose work lives we were studying framed specific activities as work. How did they convince themselves that they were working? How did they exhibit work accomplishment? What does it mean for work satisfaction or dissatisfaction to have to define a chosen and satisfying activity as "work"?

Finally, it amused us to realize, as we compared the way a potter and a principal framed their work, that we were looking at little bits of a historic process. There was a time in human history when there were no jobs. People made, hunted, planted; there were productive activities, but not, in the modern sense, work. Over many centuries, we have made activities into work. We are still doing so.

In developing the "work" theme, we began with Ronco's original organization study, but we made some deletions and additions and worked with colleagues who contributed papers that we thought would enrich our inquiry. Joan Wofford provided a profile of a school principal that expanded our "sample" to include managerial work and also helped us explore the nature of internal boundaries and the importance of products. Russ Tanner undertook a study of a food warehouse cooperative that helped us explore what happens when workers express political and social values through their work. Peter Linkow and Sharon Moriearty studied the work experience in a particularly extreme setting: a sheltered workshop for mentally retarded people.

We also worked with and supported Jon Meyer, a clinical psychologist who studied burnout. Meyer's final product did not readily fit within our outlines and thinking, but our discussions with him were influential and helpful in contributing to our understanding of stress, burnout, and the cyclical nature of work.

Donald Schon provided useful, provocative comment and feedback throughout the project.

Penelope Johnson was outstanding in her assistance with typing, production, and the overall organization of the book.

LISA PEATTIE
WILLIAM RONCO

CONTENTS

Chapter 1

MAKING WORK

Mack, the fifty-two-year-old small-boat captain, will tell you that for him fishing is "just a living, only a living." But he will also admit that he would never consider any other kind of work and has never had any other kind of job "except the army," and that fishing appeals to him because "I can be independent—no bosses."

A day on Mack's boat is exhausting: sixteen hours of baiting hooks, laying and hauling lines, and cleaning and dressing hundreds, often thousands, of pounds of fish. Or perhaps having no fish at all if it has been an unlucky day. Parts of the workday are boring in the extreme: putting bait on hooks, hauling and coiling line, traveling slowly to the fishing grounds and back. Other parts of the work are not routine enough for comfort, for even in this day of meteorology, small storms can appear unpredictably and do significant damage. Even in the relatively small port from which Mack fishes, several fishermen die each year in storms and accidents at sea.

Mack appreciates the natural beauty in ocean and sky; he will stop to watch a whale. He is proud of having and exercis-

1

ing the skill that successful fishing demands. Recently developed electronic equipment no doubt helps him make a living, but it spoils the work a little for him. He says the equipment threatens to "make anyone a fisherman."

Dan, the principal of a large high school in a wealthy suburban community, knew what he was up against when he took the job. His predecessor and his predecessor's predecessor both left a legacy of conflict and ill feeling from parents, teachers, and students alike. Thriving on the controversy, Dan immersed himself in the work. He weathered—and won—the inevitable power skirmishes and settled back to attempt to "really make the organization sing."

Dan's workday is meticulously planned well in advance. His schedule is always full, and he devotes considerable energy to filling it with tact, concern, and political acumen. He hates crises and surprises, and he uses the schedule as a weapon against management by default.

Dan likes to think of himself—and hopes others will think of him—as a scholarly manager. Savoring the smoothly running organization he has engineered, he takes on the larger issues of redefining the organization's mission. At this point, he is troubled less by surprises than by the inability of others to see and respond to his efforts.

Jeanne is a fine arts major, a sculptor and ceramic artist, but right now she is working as a production potter in her own studio. All by herself, all day long, in a low-ceilinged workroom full of gray, unfired pots, she makes mugs, one handle after another, exactly alike. Pushing herself one day, she made sixty; those were the best of all. "It is in the hands, and the more you do, the better they get. If you're going to do something like this for a living, you have to like the grungy things—like wedging clay, firing kilns. The things clay makes you do are things I like."

Jeanne's marathon, lone potting contrasts sharply with

the sociable work-world of Richard, who works in a collective studio, of which he was one of the founders. Richard started potting as a hobby while a student of architecture and planning, and only a couple of months later, he began thinking, "How many cups would I have to sell to live from this?" He still makes a living from planning, and he pots for pleasure, even though he also gets pleasure from organizing the studio and trying to push the members into selling more seriously. "I'm interested in making art more like other professions," he says. "Selling can be just as creative."

Subsequent chapters of this book explore in greater detail the work of the fisherman, the potter, the principal, and half a dozen others: managers, architects, workers in a food co-op warehouse, teachers, social workers, and participants in a sheltered workshop for the mentally retarded. We assembled this collection of "research subjects" as a means of examining the nature of work and, more specifically, work that is highly satisfying: "good work."

Our interests reflect two themes that Rosabeth Kanter identified as characterizing the ambience of work in America in the late 1970s: work as a source of self-respect and meaning, and work as a political environment, in which people demand various rights.[1]

The theme of work as a source of self-respect and meaning is a result of several major social trends: the increasing educational level of most workers, the growing proportion of younger workers, and more general attitude shifts among many workers of all ages. Younger, more educated workers, and more workers overall, expect more of work as an experience, not only as a source of economic sustenance.

[1]Rosabeth Kanter, "Work in a New America," *Daedalus: Journal of the American Academy of Arts and Sciences* 107 (Winter 1978):47–78. See also Harold L. Sheppard and Neal Q. Herrick, *Where Have All the Robots Gone?* (New York: Macmillan, 1972).

The demand that work should be satisfying seems to be a modern one. Commenting on the autobiographical documents left by nineteenth-century British working people, John Burnett noted that "For most, work was taken as given, like life itself, to be endured rather than enjoyed; most were probably glad enough to have it at all, and to expect to derive satisfaction or happiness from it was an irrelevant consideration."[2]

There are evidently many Americans for whom work today is still the necessary toil that earns a living, the daily alienation that makes possible family life and leisure enjoyment. But younger, better educated, and more affluent workers (and there are proportionately more of all of these categories) are increasingly manifesting a "concern for work as a source of self-respect and non-material reward—challenge, growth, personal fulfillment, interesting and meaningful work, the opportunity to advance and to accumulate and the chance to lead a safe, healthy life."[3]

With such increasing demands placed on the quality of the work experience, it becomes crucial to understand fully the nature of work that provides the high levels of meaning and self-respect that workers want. Reviewing the literature on work and job satisfaction, we found that most existing writing and research are not concerned with the nature of highly satisfying work. Most of what we found fits within these categories:

1. Statistical public opinion studies that document shifts in levels of job satisfaction, determinants of job satisfaction, and comparative analyses of subgroups with different levels of job satisfaction

[2]John Burnett, ed., *Useful Toil: Autobiographies of Working People from the 1820's to the 1920's* (London: Allen Lane, 1974), p. 15.
[3]Kanter, op. cit., p. 53.

2. Studies of alienation or job satisfaction in specific organizations and settings
3. Articles and books about various kinds of worker ownership schemes and job redesigns in large organizations
4. Journalistic profiles of the work experience in general

None of these approaches seems to do justice to the topic of a high-quality work experience. The statistical studies quantify something called *job satisfaction*. The journalistic profiles make it clear that *satisfaction* is a woefully inadequate term for a variety of complicated ways of getting different kinds of pleasure out of work, but these profiles usually focus on only one kind of work. The studies of worker ownership and job redesigns identify some of the characteristics of satisfying work, but always within a planned and usually a large organizational setting, where the needs of the management limit what individuals can do about their work life.

We thought we could learn something about the nature of highly satisfying work if we could examine work in "natural settings" that resemble the intentionally structured job-redesign experiments in larger corporate settings. We believed that the absence of a larger organizational environment might make it possible to observe basic principles of satisfying work uncluttered and unconstrained by bureaucratic crosscurrents and contingencies.

We chose as our research subjects people who told us that they like their work, and who work either on their own, with minimal supervision, or in small, participatory organizations. Such work situations are, of course, unusual, and not merely in being satisfying: they are unusual also in scale. Most Americans work in very large organizations.

Rosabeth Kanter provided some perspective on just how many Americans work in large organizations:

Nearly 20 percent of the total nonagricultural employed labor force works for local, state or federal government. Another 30 percent are employed by business enterprise with more than 500 people on the payroll. And this half of the labor force in government and big business does not include a variety of other large organizations that cannot be called "business" but are often increasingly run like them: private universities, private hospitals. Over 12 million Americans work in firms which employ over 10,000 people. In manufacturing, the dominance of large organizations in providing jobs is even more striking. Recently, 60 percent of all persons employed in manufacturing were in firms with at least 1,000 people, 42 percent in companies with over 10,000 employees. Over 3 million people work in firms employing over 1,000,000 people.[4]

We don't know exactly how large organizations shape the work experience. It seemed to us, however, that their very size limited the possibilities for the sort of worker autonomy and control that the research identifies as essential to high levels of job satisfaction.

Thus, we chose to study small organizations. To further ensure that the organizations we chose provided at least the structural elements of worker autonomy and control, we focused on participatory organizations: co-ops and collectives whose members have a say in governing the organization and in designing its work and theirs.

In addition to their providing the structural characteristics of satisfying work, the organizations we chose have relevance for exploring a second trend in the workplace, also identified by Kanter: the demand for worker rights. While not concerned with the traditional worker rights issues of safety or equality of opportunity, the members of the organizations we studied are quite concerned with the more general issue

[4]Ibid., p. 66.

of their rights in the workplace. Many of them came to their present work arrangements in explicit pursuit of "rights" that had eluded them at former places of work. Nearly all are dedicated to the general worker rights issue of workplace democracy.

Besides their relevance to worker rights and their provision of structural elements of job satisfaction, the organizations we studied have an intrinsic interest as examples of "hip" or "cockroach capitalism." In the United States (and it would appear elsewhere, judging by reports from France), "the desire to create, to invent, to confront reality maintains itself or even develops outside the established institutions,"[5] and individuals or small groups are making their own work situations. There are young people selling leather work along the sidewalks of Berkeley; there are cooperative restaurants; there are law and medical collectives. It is hard to know how many there are of such alternative entrepreneurs and, if it may be called a movement, how seriously to take it as such.

In any case, our interests in the politics of work have focused on the characteristics and the potential of self-employment and small participatory organizations. "Cockroach capitalists," independent self-employed work arrangements, and democratically run small businesses seem to us to offer opportunities for personal and political expression as well as a work organization more amenable to democratic operating principles than the large corporations that dominate the U.S. economy. From the outset, we have hoped that this research would provide some insights into the problems and potentials of the "small" workplace.

Our interests in the nature of highly satisfying work and the "small" workplace led us to a research design involving

[5]Jules Chancel and Pierre-Eric Tixier, "Le désir d'entreprendre," in *Et si Chacun créait son emploi?* (Paris, autrement n° 20, Sept. 1979), p. 8.

an almost anthropological study of a half-dozen workplaces: a fishing cooperative, a pottery studio, an architecture firm, a sheltered workshop, a food co-op warehouse, and several managerial jobs with a high degree of autonomy and control, for example, the principalship of a large, suburban high school. We interviewed, observed, and occasionally worked with our subjects, attempting to explore what their work is and how it is satisfying to them.

The individual chapters that follow explore the details of each kind of work. Each profile, we feel, portrays the complexity of the work and the nature of the rewards and troubles it offers.

JOB SATISFACTION

We chose the research subjects out of an interest in what is ordinarily called *job satisfaction*. We focused on people who told us they liked their work and on situations in which work seemed to have a strong potential for providing a satisfying experience.

Even more than the jobs that are redesigned to provide increased autonomy and control, the workplaces we were studying afforded workers the opportunity for much independence. Within such environments, it became apparent that the ways in which people *structure* their work life when they have the freedom to do so provide important clues to the nature of job satisfaction.

As we went on trying to understand the individuals we studied, we came to view "job satisfaction" as a dynamic *process* more than as a stable set of attitudes. The "job satisfaction" studies we read seemed to focus on the discomforts of working: monotony, boredom, safety. Herzberg[6] labeled

[6]Frederick Herzberg, *Work and the Nature of Man* (New York: Thomas Y. Crowell, 1966).

such factors "hygiene factors" several decades ago and insightfully identified them as "dissatisfiers."

We found ourselves exploring more of what Herzberg called the "satisfiers" in the work experience: features of the work experience itself rather than features in the work environment. We quickly encountered a number of predictable features of highly rewarding work among our subjects: challenge, intellectual stimulation, variety, personalization of the work, a sense of meaning of the work, and of course autonomy and control of the work.

Beyond these, we also encountered several recurring characteristics of the work experience that we did not entirely anticipate:

1. An apparent need for occasional repetition and monotony. Given the fullest breadth of choice, many of the people we studied frequently opted to work on boring, repetitive tasks that they could easily take care of in other ways. The fisherman who baits his own hooks (hundreds of them) while his crew looks on was our most poignant example.

2. An occasional, but recurring, expansion of "challenge" to out-and-out "risk." The school principal we studied—as much as the fishermen—describes his work in terms of chances taken. Such people seem to savor the risk almost as much as the ultimate outcome.

3. An interest in the public statement made by the work. All of our subjects are deeply interested in how they and their work are perceived by peers and members of their community. They do not care much about status, but they all have an *image* they hope to project.

4. Emotional ups and downs. Perhaps resulting from their internalization and personalization of the work, our subjects experienced fairly wide swings in their emotions. At the frequent high points, they could be exhilarated by and deeply pleased with their work. At the low points, they could be completely drained.

Most generally, we were surprised at the extent to which our subjects had thought through their own understanding of their work. Perhaps because of the work's fostering of autonomy and control, each person we interviewed had a well-thought-out rationale, approach, and philosophy of his or her work. Much as Robert Lane[7] found in *Political Ideology*, we discovered in a small cross section of workers an extensive body of careful thinking coupled with an appreciation of the activities and skills that consumed their working hours.

MAKING WORK

Growing out of, and somewhat beyond, any static characteristics of satisfying work we found, we were struck by the dynamic nature of job satisfaction, by the processes of making work. Our subjects' extensive autonomy in and control of their work and work organizations forces them to make work in two ways: drawing external boundaries that separate work from nonwork, and creating internal boundaries that separate and create order among all the possible ways of getting the job done.

In many instances, making work is an exercise in joy and commitment; in some cases, it is painful and difficult. The process seems to emphasize the balancing and containment of, the occasional immersion in, and the restructuring of all aspects of the work, ranging from the most abstract and intellectually enjoyable to the must uncomfortable, humiliating, and monotonous.

Much of what we see as making work has to do with drawing boundaries:

1. *Internal boundaries:* making work within work. Within

[7]Robert Lane, *Political Ideology* (New York: Free Press, 1967).

the flexibility and autonomy of their work arrangements, our subjects must create internal boundaries to organize their days, projects, and tasks. They create schedules. They create categories of different kinds of tasks and segments of the work, personal priorities and preferences. They create mechanisms that allow them to change priorities. These internal boundaries must account for and balance changing economic realities, timing, and personal desires.

2. *External boundaries:* making work distinct from nonwork. Our subjects have to separate work from nonwork activities. Emotionally invested in their work, they must make sure to make the meaning they expect the work to provide them. Surprisingly, distinguishing work from nonwork is not easy. For the fishermen, for example, what is work and what is sport? For the potters, what is hobby? The answers are not academic—to them.

For the workers we studied, there is an element of voluntarism in the activity that, by blurring the distinction between "work" and "hobby," calls into question the boundaries of the category *work* itself. The combination of these led us to examine more closely the social construction of work.

THE SOCIAL CONSTRUCTION OF WORK

The fishermen, teachers, and potters don't typically engage in debates to resolve the question "What is work?" but the issue is alive, to a degree, for all of them. In particular, they often have to answer the question when they feel that they are working too hard, when every part of their day has something to do with work. Their difficulties with the ambiguity of work as a social category signal for us a set of issues that comprise a backdrop for this research: the blurring of "work" and "hobby."

It may seem odd that as basic a social category as work is not clear. "Working" is contrasted with "fooling around," "being unemployed," "hobby," "being on welfare," "being a housewife." We need such distinctions and use them to place people socially, to determine what they are entitled to, and to decide how seriously to assess what they are doing. All this assumes that we can identify work when we see it, and that the category of work is more-or-less self-evident.

Yet a number of trends question the self-evidence of work. The demand that work be a source of respect and fulfillment, for example, suggests that work might come to resemble art or hobby. The women's movement's inquiry into the nature of housework is calling into question the extent to which that cluster of activities can be ignored as "work." The economy of the 1980s, which features an expanding service sector, is giving rise to a number of jobs (e.g., social worker) whose component tasks may more closely resemble friendly conversation than any of the more traditional occupations.

The evolution of the job structure involves a continual creation of "occupations, of 'work,' out of nonwork human activities." If "work" is activity that contributes to the production of goods and services for the market, it is plain "that activities move into the official labor force as the statuses of workers or work change [sic] due to changes in legislation and changes in the administrative rules by which membership in the official labor force is determined and legitimized."[8]What economists speak of as the expansion of the tertiary sector is in part the creation of new jobs to serve the requirements of evolving technology and institutions—computer programmers, airline attendants, customer service representatives—but also the transformation of nonmarket

---

[8]Eliot Friedson, "The Official Construction of Occupations: An Essay on the Practical Epistemology of Work" (unpublished).

human activities into "work." Thus, we have day-care workers, masseurs, group leaders, community organizers—activities that have moved into the market economy and become official occupations. Thus, the occupational categories
are man-made and changing—work descriptions cannot be
taken for granted.

Work can be seen as elicited from the individual by others, through payment, force, or persuasion; it can also be
seen as a form of self-expression. In the first aspect, it is the
cost of life; expelled from Eden, Adam was cursed by having
to earn his living by the sweat of his brow. We pay for work;
what we do by choice, unpaid, is our avocation. Societies
build systems of incentives, both positive rewards and negative sanctions, so that work will get done. But in the second
aspect, work has also been seen as man's "calling," his craft,
his means of self-expression, his way of joining with his fel-
lows in some common purpose.

All the group activities we studied—and many others—
could be pursued either as "work" or as a "hobby." Some
people fish for a living; some people fish for sport. The fishermen we studied felt superior to "sport fishermen"—but they
fished with a kind of macho zest that certainly had elements
of sport in it. Potting for many is a hobby; some of the potters
we studied actually earned a living in other ways than by
their pots. Working with children can be pursued as a volunteer effort, but the teachers we studied were extremely serious about their occupation.

The distinction between "work" and "hobby" is thus not
inherent in the activity; it lies in the social context in which
the activity is carried out. The social arrangements that structure the activity also set for it a social meaning. The same
activity may fall into the "work" or the "hobby" category,
depending not on the activity itself, but on the surrounding
social context.

What marks an activity as work?

Being paid and monetary remuneration as a prime motive for engaging in the activity certainly mark "work" off from "hobby." Being paid is, under the rules of sports, what distinguishes the amateur from the professional. But we may speak of "voluntary work," meaning an activity that is like ordinary work in every respect but payment, and for some of the people whom we came to know in this study, payment or the possibility of payment takes a secondary place to commitment to the activity. Mixed motives are general. Even the care of children by women, while motivated by affection, is surely not independent of the customary support of women by their husbands.

Sometimes "work" seems to be distinguished from "hobby" by a greater degree of commitment, by sustained effort over time. But we find that amateur actors accuse professionals of "egoistic" or "nonartistic" (i.e., less engaged) acting, and that amateur basketball players complain that their professional counterparts "don't play for the sport itself but play for the money."[9] Thus, a high level of commitment may be associated with either voluntarism or professionalism.

Work may be distinguished from leisure or hobby as being an activity that appears to be a burdensome necessity. Thus, when Peter Willmott and Michael Young discussed work and leisure with ordinary Londoners, they found that "women in overwhelming numbers regarded domestic cleaning, washing clothes and washing-up as work. These were jobs generally disliked. As for meals, routine ones were more of a drudgery than meals for guests or the great weekly ritual

[9]Robert A. Stebbins, *Amateurs: On the Margin between Work and Leisure* (Beverly Hills: Sage, 1979), pp. 73–74, 213.

of Sunday dinner."[10] On the other hand, it is clearly possible for work to be a source of gratification as well as a burden. Stevenson's *Home Book of Quotations*[11] has a long set of entries under "Work: A Curse," but it has an equally long set of entries under "Work: A Blessing." The Lewisham postman who told Willmott and Young that "I get more leisure at work that I do at home"[12] seems to have been atypical among their interviewees, chiefly in positively evaluating a working-class occupation; similar comments were not unusual among professionals. Indeed, middle-class people interviewed for the study characteristically saw in their work what the authors characterized as generally "an alliance of duty and pleasure," described in terms of a "sense of commitment."[13] Certainly, a strong positive commitment to the work activity is characteristic of the groups involved in this study. "Work" is also associated with notions of a useful product; on the other hand, a disillusioned bureaucrat who cooks, gardens, or does carpentry as a hobby may well feel that the latter are more useful than a kind of "work" seen as "processing papers."

It has also been pointed out repeatedly[14] that "work" is associated with the experience of being confined by the scheduling and disciplining of others, by loss of autonomy, and by a distribution of the product so that some persons (employers) benefit from the efforts of others (workers); this selling off or alienation of one's activity may have its experi-

---

[10]Peter Willmott and Michael Young, *The Symmetrical Family: A Study of Work and Leisure in the London Region* (London: Routledge and Kegan Paul, 1973), p. 209.

[11]Burton Stevenson, *The Home Book of Quotations* (New York: Dodd Mead, 1967).

[12]Willmott and Young, op. cit., p. 208.

[13]Ibid., p. 209.

[14]See for example the discussion in E. P. Thompson, "Time, Work—Discipline and Industrial Capitalism," *Past and Present* 38 (1967):56–97.

ential counterpart in the experience of alienation. At the same time, we recognize in the notion of self-employment that a person may be "working for himself." While at least one economist[15] sees the long hours characteristic of self-employed workers as representing pleasure in an independent working activity, the more conventional view is to treat the long hours as *self*-exploitation.

It seems that in human practice activities can become at a given moment more or less "work" or "hobby" in terms of the mental set of the persons engaging in them.

On the one hand, persons in controlled and routinized paid working situations more often than not manage to find satisfactions in the exercise of craft and initiative within the constrained situation of "the job." Unusually gifted in this, perhaps, but not atypical in making the attempt, was the cushion builder at the Ford Motor Plant interviewed by Studs Terkel:

> I could look at a job and I would do it. My mind would just click. I could stand back, look at a job, and two minutes later I can go and do it. I enjoyed the work. I felt it was a man's job. You can do something with your hands. You can go home at night and feel you have accomplished something. (Did you find the assembly line boring?) No, uh-uh. Far from boring. There was a couple of us that were hired together. We'd come up with different games—like we'd take the numbers of the jeeps that went by. That guy loses, he buys coffee.[16]

But on the other hand, a person may dignify his hobby by treating it as a sort of work, with its own place and time

[15]Tibor Scitovsky, *The Joyless Economy: An Inquiry into Human Satisfaction and Consumer Dissatisfaction* (New York: Oxford University Press, 1976), pp. 89–101.

[16]Studs Terkel, *Working: People Talk about What They Do All Day and How They Feel about What They Do* (New York: Pantheon, 1974), p. 250.

commitments. A recent study of a project for the elderly in San Francisco reports how a group of widows living in the infinite leisure of a retirement community structured part of their time as a sort of quasi-work. They met together at set hours in the common room to make craft items to sell for group projects. When one of their number proposed using for her family two of the items she had produced, the idea met with general resistance. She was taking as her private property what would otherwise be the group's, and in this way, she was breaking the frame that dignified what would otherwise be private "hobbies" by making them "work."[17]

Furthermore, in contrasting a general class of freely chosen and expressive activities we call *hobbies* with the more necessity-compelled category we call *work*, we note that there is also ambiguity in the evaluation of the two. Marx looked forward to a future in which economic necessity would no longer be the driving force behind work, so that each individual could freely choose to "do one thing today and another tomorrow, to hunt in the morning and fish in the afternoon, rear cattle in the evening, criticize after dinner, just as I have a mind"[18]; but it does not seem to have occurred to Marx to rejoice in the prospect of citizens of the new society's rejecting work altogether, for he saw people as making sense of their lives only in being "productively active." In proposing a distinction between "labor," which arises in the realm of necessity and serves to reproduce human life, and "work," which creates a true product, Hannah Arendt drew on a long (and one might well argue class- and sex-biased) tradition of invidious comparison between the creative activity of the lei-

---

[17] Arlie Russell Hoschschild, *The Unexpected Community* (Englewood Cliffs, N.J.: Prentice-Hall, 1973), p. 42.

[18] Karl Marx and Friedrich Engels, "The German Ideology," excerpted in Lewis S. Feuer, *Basic Writings on Politics and Philosophy: Karl Marx and Friedrich Engels* (Garden City, N.Y.: Doubleday, 1959), p. 254.

sured classes and the servile work of the masses,[19] but this tradition has in Western thought its own antithesis: the Protestant Ethic strain that sees useful work as central to ethical practice as a human being.[20]

At the same time that alienation through wage labor debases work, respect is given to work as the serious business of life because in the monetized society, it acquires exchange value. Thus, at the same time that our work groups try to make work less like a job and more like a hobby, we also see them giving the activity more weight by making it more economically serious. For example, one of the members of the potters' collective says that if the group would organize to sell collectively and to sell more, they would work harder and better.

It thus turns out that the categories of "work" and "hobby" are fuzzy categories. They are not defined by the inherent nature of the task to be performed. They are not defined by a clear differentiation of the motives with which the activity is performed. Nor is there an evaluative standard that clearly differentiates the two.

This set of ambiguities is hardly captured by the concept of *job satisfaction* on which most work studies are focused. The concept of *job satisfaction* seems to imply a taking-for-granted of the separation between "work" and "hobby" that we see as an underlying issue for all of the groups we have been examining. It is not simply the relative balance of utilities and disutilities, and of compensation for disutility with reference to a clear category, but the categories themselves that are at issue.

[19]Hannah Arendt, *The Human Condition* (Garden City, N.Y.: Doubleday, 1959).
[20]See Max Weber, *The Protestant Ethic and the Spirit of Capitalism* (New York: Scribner, 1930) and R. H. Tawney, *Religion and the Rise of Capitalism* (Magnolia, Mass.: Peter Smith, 1926).

Each of the work groups we have been studying has in one way or another been structured so as to make it possible for the members to maximize the "hobby" aspects of the occupation in the sense of leaving the worker free to structure, to create, to play. But the organizations are also structured to make the activity—which, as we have said, could in other circumstances be a "hobby"—function as work. The way in which members of these groups structure their work, as well as their own commitment to it, makes the activity sit right across the structural ambiguities of the boundary between "work" and "hobby." Thus, our attention to these work groups turns out to be attention not only to work satisfaction and work commitment, but to the social construction of work itself.

INHERENT DILEMMAS OF "GOOD WORK"

It is no doubt a sort of triumph to construct for oneself a satisfying work situation. But it turns out that good work has some inherent dilemmas.

It is important for people—some of them, anyway, and the people we came to know are among them—to have work that they can feel positively committed to. Good work for these people is work they *want* to do, work they do for more than the money. But committed work is hard to limit. Because the workers are in it for more than the money, they find themselves at it outside of working hours, and putting in more energy than they would have to hold the job. Though they may not at the time be able or willing to predict it, the result may be burnout.

For example, a number of the people who were most active in organizing a school we studied, where teachers managed and made policy, put in a year or two of furious energy and then left the school altogether for other, usually much less demanding, positions. The school, now running with people who work without the passion of the early days, has a tamer feeling to it.

A second dilemma has to do with the flip side of burn-out: Good work is flexible enough to allow people to withdraw as they feel the need. This flexibility is not only convenient and pleasant, it also enables workers to feel that engagement is voluntary. But to feel that an activity is serious (i.e., work rather than play), the worker needs to feel a sense of necessity. The fishermen we studied set their own days and hours for an activity that for other people out in the same bay in similar boats is "sport." The fishermen we studied make much of the difference between themselves and the sportfishermen: for them, fishing is a living, an economic necessity.

The potters we studied work intermittently and spend a good deal of their "working day" in chatting with each other and watering the plants. Their commitment to the studio as an organization is important in part because it represents a serious commitment to potting as work.

A third dilemma is that good work allows for people to be creative and inventive. However, there can be some real satisfaction in repetition and boredom. The repetitive fishing work of baiting and winding and cleaning the fish gives a satisfying rhythm for dependable routine in an environment where uncertainty can often be an enemy. Good work involves variety and surprise—but also the repetition and limitation that make it possible for the worker to acquire and exercise specialized skill. A young potter, making mug after identical mug, twelve hours a day in her studio, and a gifted teacher who all day long allows herself no moment of undisciplined response, no span in inattention—these are two very different kinds of work and worker. But they are alike in their solitary pride in the exercise of disciplined skill.

Good work is work that can be made, shaped, formed by the workers themselves, that can be an extension of their will to create. But a fourth dilemma is that making work can be a burden; the worker has to make the decisions and provide continuing initiative. The fishermen like very much the fact that no one orders them to come to work—the decision each day is their own. But making that decision every day means forcing oneself up out of bed, usually in the dark, and entering the world of the noisy, lurching boat. The principal and the teacher in the worker-controlled school spend a good chunk of their Sundays planning their work for the coming week. This teacher is justly proud of the way in which she has organized her class so that all day every day, the children carry out learning activities in varying sizes of groups with appropriate materials. But to make that happen requires endless ongoing planning, and that seems to hedge against the sort of spontaneity that both she and the children might enjoy.

A fifth dilemma arises particularly in work with people— a growing category, as the increasing size of the service sector suggests. Close interactions with other people add a dimension of warmth and sociability and have the potential to enhance even otherwise boring jobs. But people work often leaves no clearly visible output and may leave workers wondering if they are performing well. Persons intensely committed to effectively carrying out people work (the school principal in the following chapters, for example) may not have an empirical, objective confirmation of their effectiveness. In the absence of such measures, they have to make them themselves—another dimension of making work.

A final dilemma has to do with a worker's ability in

"good" work to express her or his values and politics. The dilemma is that while good work offers this possibility, it may take some additional difficult steps to realize the potential. Political expression implies some interaction with others; individual self-employment efforts have limited ability to make a strong symbolic political statement. Working in a group, however, almost inevitably entails compromises, and compromises may comprise a worker's original political interests. Furthermore, making participation function requires another kind of effort that may be experienced as a burden, rather than as freedom.

These dilemmas are evident in varying degrees in the profiles that follow. What may not be so clear is their close connection with out notion of *making work*. Each of the dilemmas is a balancing-act, "good" aspect of work that needs to be constrained and molded in order to be fully enjoyed. As far as we could see from our research subjects, "job satisfaction" depends on resolving these dilemmas with grace and inventiveness.

The internal structuring of work—schedules, tasks, coordination, placing in space—is not independent of the external boundaries that set off work from nonwork. There is always an implicit audience. The meaning of work, which we refer to usually by the term *job satisfaction*, is both personal and social. The potters arguing about whether they should present themselves on their card as a pottery collective or as a studio are arguing both about the social setting of their activity and about its meaning, and therefore its structuring, to themselves. The fishermen taking pride in their macho individualism do so against an implicit background of the regimented work of the factory or the white shirt and the bureaucratic order of the office. Thus, those who are free to structure their work in their own way are engaged in a complex process on both the societal and the individual level. They do not have the job as a shell into which they fit. They do not just go to work; they make their work. In so doing, they may suggest something of what the social construction of work involves for us all.

Chapter 2

FISHING WORK

Some 240 boats fish commerically from the Cape Cod port of Barnham. They range from the "mosquito fleet" of roughly a hundred one-man boats that can go out only in good weather, to boats of 50 feet carrying a small crew. None, however, can go out for a week at a time, like the big boats one finds in other New England ports, because of the sandbar at the end of the harbor. This sandbar, treacherously shifting its location with the weather, prevents the passage of deep-draft vessels.

The port is beautiful, a cornerstone of the town's salty white and wooden-shingled ambience. The town's beauty has helped to attract a retired community whose wealth contrasts with the predominantly blue-collar natives. Belying the town's apparent serenity, the natives and retirees are in frequent and heated conflict over town spending, regulation, and taxation. The conflicts overlay their deeper jealousies and beliefs concerning the privileges and rights of ownership, money and history.

The economic contrasts are perhaps most pointed at the fish pier itself, located almost in the middle of the town's poshest resort. With the same spirit they bring to tennis and golf matches, the tourists stroll from the immaculate resort cottages to the pier to watch the fishermen unload their catch. Many of them are unaware that the resort carries the same name as the sandbar that often claims several boats—and fishermen's lives—each year.

In many ways, fishing work in Barnham is like fishing work from any port: difficult, often unprofitable and tedious—yet also romantic: Man the Hunter, captain (literally) of his destiny. Classic examples of macho autonomy, fishing boat owners have a special ability to control and define their work. A fisherman in his early forties, formerly an accountant, explained, "The appeal is freedom. You do as you damn please. It's the last frontier."

The sandbar that limits boat size helps make Barnham fishermen an especially independent and autonomous group. The bar has made Barnham a port of small boats, a place where the local economy is geared to be responsive to small-boat owners and operators. With more small boats, there are proportionately more boat *owners* in Barnham, and hence more people who can call the shots and do as they "damn please." The boats that do have crews don't have large ones, and the small crews tend to be more independent, informal, and collegial than the crews on larger boats.

Even in Barnham, though, the inherent independence of fishermen is incomplete. To fish for a living in any port is to confront the economic realities of technology and markets. Boats cost from a thousand dollars for a used skiff to seventy thousand dollars for a new, larger boat, unequipped. A bigger boat makes possible a bigger catch. It also makes a bigger catch necessary, to pay for it, and it brings with it a need for a crew and other equipment. Modern fishing equipment enhances productivity but represents a need for more capital—around ten thousand dollars for depthfinder–fishfinder, L.O.R.A.N., radios, radar.

Bigger boats and sophisticated electronic gear can strengthen their owner's independence, but not always. They may necessitate personal debts, which themselves impose limits and pressures, and they often involve extra maintenance work as well. Moreover, some tools that are meant to improve the productivity of fishing alter the nature of fishing work. The electronic gear, for example, takes away some of the adventure and sense of the skill—and the *feeling* of independence—that keeps the element of sport in fishing for a living. One fisherman says, "Fishing used to be sporting, not so methodological. These days we have a lot of electronic operators—very few fishermen."

Nor do the economics of the fishing industry often support the independence of fishermen. In many cases, the fisherman who can do as he pleases at sea is quite dependent on a limited number of local buyers (some ports have only one buyer) to pay a reasonable sum for his catch.

Barnham fishermen, like their counterparts in some other ports, have taken steps to minimize the inequities of fishing economics and gain some control over that aspect of their work. In 1966, a group of them, some of whom took out mortgages to raise the money, bought out one of the local fish buyers, with his ice plant, building, and trucks, and turned the business into a co-op. Through the co-op, fishermen better control the sales of their own fish and avoid fattening the wallet of a middleman buyer. Only about half of the town's several hundred fishermen actually belong to the co-op, but nearly all the fishermen agree that the co-op's presence "keeps other buyers honest."

Belonging to or having been accepted by the co-op is one way, fishermen feel, of showing that you're serious. They also enjoy the sociability attached to belonging. At the same time, they somewhat resent the time it takes to supervise the running of the co-op's business and are stingy in letting the

co-op have much capital to operate with. Personal involvement in the co-op, while necessary to make the organization
work, threatens the fishermen's ability to come and go as
they please. And financing the co-op properly, though it
makes sound business sense, feels too much like imposed
charity.

The co-op is by no means a final solution to the fishermen's economic plight. The market for seafood is unstable,
and its instability affects fishermen directly—all the co-op
does is to limit exploitation in a difficult system. In some
ways, the co-op is like the town's harbormaster, moving the
marker buoys each week to keep up with the treacherously
shifting channel.

Barnham fishermen hold mixed views of the co-op, and
of nearly every topic we discussed with them. Contrary to
popular belief, they were not at all unwilling to talk about
their work. Several were even willing to have me come
aboard and help out—a researcher's fantasy.

One of the fishermen who took us aboard is a longtime
co-op member, a past president and founder. The other fishermen are not members and hold differing views regarding
the co-op's effectiveness. The co-op member resembles most
of his peers: a long-liner, an older (over forty-five) man, and
owner of one of the larger (about forty-foot) boats. The other
fishermen are younger and pursue their work in smaller craft.

LONG-LINING

"Long-lining," or "line trawling," involves laying a
longline along the ocean floor. The line has hundreds of
baited hooks and is marked and set at both ends by an anchor
and an iridescent, medicine-ball-sized buoy. The line is kept
in premeasured lengths of about 600 feet, coiled neatly in

tubs placed carefully in the boat. Each tub has about 200 hooks, spaced several feet apart from each other on the line. A boat usually carries between five and fifteen tubs, but ten or twelve tubs' worth of long-lining usually amounts to a full workday.

The work of long-lining has mostly to do with tending the line: paying it out from the tubs so that it sinks to the bottom untangled; then retrieving the line with the fish—the fishermen hope—attached. In the paying out and the retrieving, the line must be kept in order. Snags delay the process, stop the boat, and ultimately limit the number of fish that can be caught. At day's end, the line must be coiled and readied for the next trip.

Work begins minutes after the boat leaves the town pier (several hours before sunrise) with the baiting of the hooks. It's a gray, humid morning. Very early. Humidity collects in drops on the decks, the roofs, mixes with the occasional wave that splashes over the gunwale. The boat is gray also, its wooden parts dulled by a salt patina. The few items of color stand out disproportionately: pink marker buoys, yellow rubber overalls, silver beer cans. Riding low, the boat seems more a part of the water than a pleasure boat would be. Water comes in and is used to clean the decks. Even so, the forty-foot boat seems more substantial than a pleasure craft of equal length.

Mack, the captain and owner of the boat, and Frank, his crew, each take up a tub and begin uncoiling the line. They bait each hook with a piece of squid, and they reset and straighten the boat hooks with a wooden form attached to a bulky wooden index-finger ring. They proceed one hook at a time, taking great care to coil the line neatly after they have baited the hooks. Mack's teenage son Larry pilots the boat. Larry is "extra" crew for the summer. Though the three don't converse, they seem to enjoy each other's company.

Mack has been president of and served on the board of directors for the fishing co-op. Active in the co-op since its start, Mack believes, as do many of the established fishermen in town, that the co-op is a necessity. He serves in the co-op because he believes that it takes active involvement on the part of members to make the co-op work. "It has to be that way," he contends.

A thick, blackened pipe carries the exhausts from the motor amidships up through the cabin roof to a muffler, but little seems muffled. The whole boat roars, clangs, bangs, and vibrates. Conversation is all but impossible. The noise is worst at the stern, out from under the cabin roof. It is quietest below decks, but little work is done there. In the area where the baiting is done, conversation can occur only if one is willing to shout. Most communication is nonverbal, and even that is limited. The engine is hardly muffled, they say, because it is "more efficient."

The boat is highly personalized, filled with gadgets and equipment. A rusty horseshoe hangs askew over the engine, supplementing the boat's full stock of electronic gear: radar, fishfinder–depth-measure, and L.O.R.A.N.-C. The high-tech electronics mix oddly with the hooks and the horseshoe, and with Mack and Frank using wooden hook rings, baiting in the background. Below decks, Dramamine is prominent on the shelves, the shiny packs jutting out from the oil, bread, candy, beer and cigarettes, maple syrup, and dish detergent. There is an oil-fired stove with a blower pump; it looks as if it could heat a small gymnasium. Stove and domestic equipment have doors or railings to keep their contents from sliding out. Several large green coolers hold iced bait, but one— as big as the others—holds food and beer. There is no head, but the paper towels wedged in at the gunwale are printed in flowers. The boat literally does the work of fishing, pulling in the lines with hydraulic power drawn off the engine.

The work area is open on all sides, but there are catches, slots, and hinges all around to enclose the area when the New England winter settles in. As with the shelves below decks, things all seem to fit together neatly. It is possible to enclose the entire work area except for a small, hinged flap that incoming hooked fish can push out of the way.

The boat is work, home, and the protection of the fishermen's very lives. It is an instrument, a tool, and a toy, too. (When the owner of a smaller boat asked me if I'd like to pilot "her," he knew he was giving me a gift, a funny kind of amusement park ride.) Also, the boat is an investment and equity. Fishermen get increasingly larger boats as they continue to work, and when they retire, the boat may be their pension.

THE GROUNDS

We noisily steam to the fishing grounds, out through the harbor, the breakwater, and, quickly, out of sight of land. Mack and Frank hit a rhythm in their baiting. They finish a few tubs and replace the coffee (blood-curdling stuff produced in an aluminum pot on the galley stove) with a beer. At 8 A.M., with much of the work behind them, and twenty miles out of port, they loosen up a bit. Larry disappears belowdecks for a brief nap, and Mack now takes an occasional break from baiting to check the course. There is more conversation now, Mack and Frank shouting at each other genially.

Conversation stops suddenly when Mack spots a whale a few hundred yards to starboard. He slows the boat, and we all take a few minutes to watch the whale swim by. There is nothing to say or do, only to watch this miraculous creature, this apartment building of a fish crash, splash, spew, and spout past.

It takes two and a half hours to reach the grounds—a smooth, submerged plateau that rises above the surrounding, deeper ocean floor. Mack finds the spot by instinct but then checks his L.O.R.A.N.-C to pinpoint the position. "After thirty years of this, I just know," he reflects. We steam slowly over the plateau until Mack gets a promising reading on the fishfinder, and then the line goes in. Frank tosses the buoy, Larry pitches the anchor, and they both stand back watchfully, staring at the line paying out of the tub through a metal chute over the stern. Each hook clicks through the chute, Frank holding a broom handle ready to wedge into any tangles that may appear.

Here is more mixing of high technology and low. The "spot" is found with the sensitive electronic fishfinder, which line-inks the depth on a role of graph paper. Thick, low peaks on the graph are usually fish. The fish located, hand-baited hooks and lines are thrown in, anchored by faded buoys and sinkers made of the kind of weights used for window sash ropes.

It takes several hours to pay out all the line, the boat always moving. We set three triple tubs close together, then steam ten minutes or so to another spot to set the last triple tub. As soon as we set the last tub, we return to the first line to begin to pull the fish in. With all the line out, there is another noticeable drop in tension on the boat: there is no further need for concern about the outgoing line's getting tangled.

HAULING THE LINE

Now, the tension has become suspense: What will we pull in? Mack hits a valve on "Hydro-Slave" and the hydraulic wheel turns, pulling the line in with the roller. Frank catches it at the left side of the boat and begins to coil it. The taut line brings up the first dozen or so hooks, coming up as they went in, empty, except for the bait. Mack hits the hooks with the club end of his gaff to pop the bait off. Finally, the first fish comes into view—a medium-sized cod. Larry hooks it under the gill with a gaff hook attached to a broom handle. He slides it into the compartment he has walled off between the engine and the gunwale, behind Mack.

Larry is wearing waist-high heavy boots and standing inside a wooden box within the larger wooden landing box. Fish keep coming: small, large, medium cod; pollock; haddock. Quickly there are a dozen fish flopping around, several hundred pounds altogether. The hauler keeps the line taut, coming steadily. Mack checks to make sure he's not bringing it in too fast for Frank, but Frank is fine. He stands and coils, unsnagging the hydraulic wheel occasionally. The pile of fish increases.

The rhythm goes steadily with only a few interruptions, and the breaks don't last long. One thing that slows down the beat is the appearance of an ocean catfish on the line. Bull-headed, blue, and with cartoon-character protruding teeth, the catfish sends Larry quickly to a safe corner of the box. "They'll go for your feet," Frank explains, and sure enough, this one, though stunned by its quick trip up from the ocean floor, flops over and sinks its teeth deeply into a large cod. Mack notes, "They eat shellfish."

After the first catfish, others don't break the rhythm so much. Larry flings them to the back of the box, then leans back overboard, ready to gaff the next cod. His movements are machinelike and slow. Every single hook must be dealt with: either the bait or the fish must be removed.

The pulling in continues for hours, with only these interruptions: to retrieve a fish that slipped off the gaff, to untangle the line from the hydraulic puller, and to move from the end of the one line to the beginning of another. There is a brief pause when some sharks are spotted. Some of the incoming cod have *Jaws*-like bites taken out of their abdomens.

Though there are no interruptions, other things go on while the line comes in. Everyone manages to put away a few sandwiches and beers. People start translating the catch into dollars. The CB chatter begins to include news of the prices being paid that day for fish brought back to the pier.

Variations

The first three triple tubs have brought in a reasonably large amount of fish, but the last is a disaster. Bait keeps coming back, and the few fish on the line are very small. Mack remarks, "It's irritating as hell when you're not getting any fish." Mack points out that it's always this risky. He feels lucky that he set the three lines in a productive spot. Ten minutes of travel made all the difference, and he had almost put the three triple tubs where he had set the one unproductive one.

There is little time to make sense of all this, though, for we must get back to port to make the evening truck run to the big city fish markets. If we don't make it, the fish will still be salable but will have lost the edge of freshness that adds to their market value.

Dressing

As we head back to port, a whole new phase of work begins: dressing the fish. Perhaps because this is unpleasant work, there seems to be less enthusiasm all around. Perhaps, also, the lack of enthusiasm is simply a product of fatigue. We have already put in an eight-hour day, and although today's twelve hours are less than the usual schedule, there is ample reason for us to be worn out.

Frank continues to work on coiling the line while Mack and Larry work at different dressing chores. First, Mack cuts the fish. He makes three cuts: two of them form a V behind the gills; the third begins at the top of the V and slashes down the length of the fish's belly. The procedure sounds clinical, but it's approximate and messy. With the bigger fish, he make a few extra cuts and decapitates them.

The cods' heads go in a box atop the engine, to be used later for bait. The slit fish are passed on to Larry. Mack, enjoying the rhythm of the work, occasionally throws a fish back with more force than he needs to, adding to the slop surrounding Larry. Larry, however, is not very sensitive to this mess. His job all along has been to reach into the abdominal slit, pull out the entrails, and throw them overboard.

Dressing takes nearly half the trip back in, and it leaves the boat with blood and gore on walls, cabin ceiling, windshield—everything. When the last fish has been cleaned, Larry washes down the boat. Jack scrubs all the dirtied surfaces with a stiff brush, and within a half hour, the boat is as clean as ever.

KNOWING

The fish are now packed in a box amidships, and we finally have some free time. Mack cooks up some cod tongues—the soft, boneless triangle of flesh below the mouth—in flour and margarine. He serves them on a paper bag, on the engine cover, with salt, Wonder Bread, and what must be the sixth or seventh beer of the day. He says, "I'll bet you never had that before." He's right, and the cod tongue is superb.

Philosophizing, Mack says fishing work is "just a living, only a living." He likes it very much, would never consider leaving, and has never had any other job, "except the army."

He fishes about 130 days a year and earns a substantial living. He likes the work because he can be "independent, no bosses." Also, he likes the sea.

Despite his commitment to the co-op, Mack places it well behind the work of fishing in his own set of personal priorities. Fishing work is fishing, after all, not marketing or organization building. The independence, craft, mastery, and mystery of fishing don't mix with a concern for marketing.

He takes me below and reviews the nautical charts, pointing out where we have been (about twenty miles offshore) and where some other good spots are. He explains the various electronic gear: the fishfinder–depthfinder reads the depth under the boat and signals the presence of fish; radar, especially helpful in a fog, shows the presence of other boats 360 degrees around his boat. The newest piece of equipment, L.O.R.A.N.-C, gives latitude and longitude readings so accurate that it is possible to pinpoint a spot on the ocean "within fifty yards." This information is most helpful in returning to productive spots at sea.

Other fishermen resent the electronics because they "make anybody a fisherman." Mack is less negative. He feels that electronic equipment helps to make the work safer, and he's glad to have it. He is quick to point out, though, that he uses it only as backup. Intuition and "just knowing" come first.

To Mack, "knowing" is important. He takes special pride in long-lining—as opposed to jigging—because of its demands for skill. "It doesn't take anything upstairs to go jigging," he remarks. Long-lining is more complex, it takes more knowledge. (People who go jigging see lots of problems with long-lining, but more about that later.) Knowledge is also important because it gives power in a kind of work where power is everything, but knowledge has limits. Mack explains, for example, that "Fish seem to eat more at slack tide, so we need to get out to the grounds when the tide is slow. . . . Sometimes we pay attention to that, but sometimes we don't. There's also the force of the tide, and a lot of things you just feel." Factual knowledge and skill must be supplemented by intuition.

The mastery of fishing is understated, perhaps because it demands extreme amounts of physical work. It makes for a tiring day, and the days are typically sixteen to twenty-two hours long. But as the length of a workday is extreme, the fishermen are quick to point out that they don't go out every day, but "only" about 130 days a year. In other words, there is mastery and control in their choice, each day, of whether to put out to sea.

CAPTAIN AND CREW

Mastery and independence also figure in captain–crew and captain–captain relations. In a formal sense, the working arrangements for the crew are quite oppressive. The captain is in charge: he sets the pace, makes the decisions. The crew's job is to follow orders. The crew's income, which is typically a share of the boat's income, depends entirely on the captain's ability to find fish.

The crew has more power than one might suppose, however. Working at close quarters places a premium on working things out, and it is to the captain's benefit to have a standing relationship with his crew. Standing relationships minimize the possibility of missed days' work and have other payoffs as well: a standing crew can be expected to work harder at sea, to take more of an interest in the boat, and even to work on the boat during the winter.

Mack seems concerned about his crew, checking with Frank frequently to make sure he isn't bringing the line in too fast for Frank to coil it. Frank has the run of the boat. He does

the work that must be done, but he also takes breaks, lux-
uriating in sitting back and staring at the horizon.

When we land at the dock, however, the lines separating
captain and crew reemerge. Mack heads for the weighing
room, where he can get a quick estimate on the day's income,
while Frank hoses the boat down. And when Mack has finally docked the boat, he goes out for a few beers with some
other captains. In the bar, the crew members huddle at a
separate table.

JIGGING

In the predawn gray glow, we don't quite need the boat's
spotlights to sight the marker buoys as we follow the channel
out of the harbor. Going jigging now and then, there is much
more of a sense that one is fishing, not operating machinery.
The boat is smaller and faster than Mack's. Because it's smaller, the engine is mounted astern, instead of amidships as on
Mack's boat. Much of the noise astern does not stay in the
boat; it is relatively quite, and conversation is possible.

Fred is extremely proud of the boat. It has been his now
for three weeks, a vast improvement over his former craft.
This boat is twenty-eight feet long, with a small cuddy and
roof over the wheel; his other boat was an open twenty-two
foot skiff. This one is clean, fast, and quiet and is equipped
with all the available electronic gear. It has little design touch-
es: nooks and crannies well placed, space where space should
be. This is understandable because it was built by another
fisherman.

In some ways, Fred's boat is a scaled-down version of
Mack's: many of the parts and the gear are in evidence out in
the open. But there are some obvious differences, too. Mack
has a large, industrial rubber mat to stand on at the wheel;

Fred's mat is smaller, faded, and more slippery, and it has a faded Cadillac insignia in its corner. Most noticeably, the gear for jigging is less complicated than for that for long-lining. With jigging, there are no bait, bait boxes, tubs, buoys, or anchors decorating the deck.

In the smaller boat one is much closer to, more a part of the sea. The ride of the boat, though quieter, is much more jumpy. Fred tells me how he always used to get seasick on his smaller boat: "You throw up, but you have to keep at it." He hasn't yet been sick on his new boat.

Without the need to bait up, we have a leisurely trip to the fishing grounds. Fred and I chat while George goes below to catch up on some sleep. Not regular crew, George owns a boat that is "in the shop." Crewing with Fred for a few weeks has been good for George because Fred has had an exceptionally good week, "the best week of my life." He has brought in over a thousand dollars worth of fish, "so I could pay off all my debts." It's also been good for Fred to have George around. George is reliable and competent, a relatively rare find as crew for the skipper of a small boat. Experienced crew usually prefer to ship on larger boats, where the share is likely to bring in more money.

Fred has only recently begun to take on any crew, preferring to work alone in order not to have to "be bothered." Fred describes himself as a classic sort of lone fisherman: "I used to go out in all kinds of weather in my skiff. I'd go out even when the big boats stayed in. I took a lot of chances, but that's what you have to do in order to make any money."

Fred earned a reputation for being a hustler, and the reputation included his preference for working alone. "When you work alone," he points out, "you don't have any hassles about coming and going, or about doing accounting work for paying people. You're really independent, and it's easier to find fish, too. You can concentrate better. You can think."

Lately Fred has taken on crew "because without some-body else to talk to out here, it's incredibly lonely. I used to talk to the fish, to the boat, to the gulls—to anything. I have crew mostly for my mental health, for some company. They add something to what I catch, but I don't usually make money off the deal. Sometimes I even lose money, but it's worth it for the company."

Generally, jigging seems a less encumbered operation than long-lining, but within jigging, there are different issues of complexity, such as crew and boat size. A bigger boat is safer, quieter, more stable, and more comfortable, but it also costs more to maintain, and there is more at stake in its use. "With the skiff you never had to worry," Fred recalls. "I could clear the breakwater, leave the harbor anytime. Now, with the bigger boat, I have to watch out for the tides; I can't come or go at low tide. And if I run aground, I could lose a whole lot of money."

Money is more a part of discussions with Fred than it was with Mack. Fred's situation is less stable, more variable. He is still basking in the success of his thousand-dollar week, but he is also quick to point out that "It can't continue like that. Besides, it didn't make me rich, only helped me pay off some debts, and I have a lot of them."

As we clear the breakwater, a sports fisherman eases in behind us and begins to follow. Crisscrossing over the wave like a waterskier, his shiny multicolored fiberglass boat con-trasts with our clean, but dull, gray one. Fred spots him and begins pounding his fist on the railing over the wheel. "They say fishermen are crude," Fred observes. "It's not us, though. It's those guys—the sports fishermen. That guy [he motions to the boat behind us] followed us all around yester-day. I couldn't believe it. Finally, I just went up to him and asked him what the hell he was doing. I told him. 'This is my living! You just come around and fish the spots that I find. It's only sport to you, but it's my living.' He went away, but I thought he might be back.''

The sports fishermen quickly does clear out, but he is replaced by a more difficult presence: fog. The stuff rolls in thick puffs as we cross a breakwater, immersing us and cutting off visibility. Fred wakes George and brings him, still a little groggy, to the radar. We don't drop speed at all, but George now keeps watch on the radar screen for possible collisions with other boats. Initially, there is a lot of tension. The fog is so thick that one can't see more than twenty feet in front of the boat, and the boat's engine is too noisy for us to hear boats nearby. More than a simple danger, the fog is spooky, and Fred's stories round out the picture. He goes on about how, several years ago, he nearly rammed a tanker on a day like this.

Yet, after a bit of this, the tension lessens. We make visual contact with some boats that had been on the radar. Occasionally, George punches Fred on the arm, Fred cuts the engine, and we listen apprehensively for an oncoming boat that the radar has picked up. Though we can "see" them (mostly by listening, and we can't be sure of exactly where they are), we can be even less sure they can see us, so Fred panics a few times when a boat gets close. At one point, he dashes to the stern, jumps on the gunwale, waves his arms, and shouts through the pea soup at an oncoming engine noise, "Stop! You're going to ram us!" They miss us narrowly, and Fred comes back to the wheel, muttering to himself.

FRED

Fred is one of the younger breed of fishermen in town. He began five years ago when he found that his college degree in biology did not get him any kind of job that appealed to him. He tried crewing, then moved on to buying his own small skiff, forsaking biology completely. "Once you get fishing in your blood, you're stuck," he observes.

Fred likes fishing but is very vocal with complaints, too. His complaints don't deal so much with the work of fishing as with conditions in the port and in New England in general. His biggest complaint is that "Social life here stinks. There are no women. Oh, there are a few in the summer, but in the winter, it's a desert." The winter itself is a bad time. Fishing is impossible because of the weather and no one else is in town. "I have to travel in the winter, or else go crazy," he remarks.

Fred is clearly at a different stage of his career than Mack is. However, it is not clear that Fred wants to end up in a position like Mack's. For one thing, he prefers jigging work to long-lining. He crewed on some long-liners and hated the noise and the machinery. He likes the simplicity of jigging, even if it is not as profitable. He has equipment on board for several longline tubs (he would have to haul these by hand, since he doesn't have a Hydro-Slave), but he seldom uses it. Fred is aggressive in looking for the fish, but he's out to have a good time, too. He's on the CB frequently, making contact with friends, seeing where everyone else is.

SILENCE

After long-lining, this is the very picture of simplicity. We zigzag for a bit, George and Fred checking the fishfinder for blips. When they find them, Fred cuts the engine and we drift. The silence is overpowering, and Fred is quick to point out that it is this silence that makes jigging better than long-lining.

Fred gets the line out and helps me locate and try on an extra pair of rubber boots, overalls, and gloves. Meanwhile, George already has his line in the water. He has taken up a small plywood board, about a foot square, that has the line wrapped around it. At one end of the line is the jig: a large, metal lure, a silver minnow with a menacing hook. Several feet up from the jig is a plastic worm on another hook, and several feet from that is another worm and hook.

To get started, all George has done is to take off about a hundred feet of the heavy monofilament line—just enough to reach the bottom at this point—and pitch it overboard. As soon as the jig hits bottom, he pulls it up so that it is a few feet above the ocean floor and safe from getting snagged. Then he "jigs"; that is, he yanks the line up and lets it sink back down.

As George gets a bite and pulls in the first fish, we all get more excited than we could have on Mack's boat, where the machine did the work. George struggles, speculates, and struggles some more, finally landing the fish. This particular fish is a rarity, a bluefish, and one that puts up a fight. George and Fred agree they haven't seen one of these in a while. George cleans and dresses it immediately because bluefish tend to spoil fast, and perhaps also because he has his eye on it. "They're awfully good," he says several times.

Fred and George are bringing in cod. Unlike the machine in Mack's boat, there are plenty of small interruptions. Each fish is remarked on and sized up, even before it comes on board. Trying to judge from the strength of the pull on the line, Fred and George guess if the fish will be a "marker" (a small one) or a "steaker" (one big enough to cut into steaks). They are fairly quick about landing fish, gaffing them so they won't fall off the hook ("Cod have weak mouths," George explains). The lines are back in the water as soon as the fish is landed, and by the time, the fish are set in the box, the line has sunk to a depth right for more jigging.

Each fish is an event. We're all pulling in fish, jigging at our own rhythms and hauling the caught cod the hundred feet to the surface. The hauling is odd: it makes the work more like farming than fishing in the way it's done for sport. The cod don't fight; sometimes, they even seem to swim along, docilely, to the boat.

After perhaps ten fish, the trouble begins. George snags Fred's line, and although George does not lose the fish he's bringing in, Fred loses "bottom time." George snags his line: the curls of monofilament entwine themselves in each other, and he stands in the stern, cursing their unwieldiness. I catch what I first take to be the ultimate steaker, but it is the bottom, and I lose the jig trying to bring the line back.

We've been in this spot only about a half hour, but Fred says, "Let's go." George has anticipated Fred's call and has already pulled in his line. We speed for five or ten minutes, then slow down. Fred and George once again eyeing the fishfinder. After a few minutes, they nod. Fred cuts the engine, and our lines go over again.

DENNY

The voice of a friend of Fred's, Denny, booms in on the CB. Fred and he chat for a bit; then Fred asks if he'd like to have an extra crew. Within a few minutes, Denny's boat appears, guided by compass headings provided by Fred. He pulls up alongside, and I make the transfer, worrying that if I fall in, the rubber boots will fill with water and drag me quickly to a briny death.

Denny's boat is to George's boat as George's is to Mack's: smaller, faster, more sparse, more dangerous, closer to the sea. It is a twenty-two-foot fiberglass open skiff with a control console amidships. There is no cabin, just boxes for fish built in front of the console and a few little cubbies for food, bait, and odds and ends.

Denny's boat has a "small V-8." As he takes off, I must

sit or be knocked down by the pounding and slipping. He steers into the clearing fog, eyes not ahead but on the fishfinder, and we speed along for about fifteen minutes before he cuts the engine. Still glued to the fishfinder, he zigzags a few times and then kills the engine. "This looks worth a try," he announces and tosses his line over. I toss in one from the bow, and we are in business.

Almost instantly, the fish begin to bite, and we pull the lines in hand-over-fist to find fish on two or three hooks on each line. Markers and steakers, too, are coming up, a bonanza of fish. Though we hardly know each other, Denny and I get goofy and silly over what's happening. We quickly bring in about a dozen fish before they stop. Dead. "That's the way it goes," Denny observes, and we are off to another spot.

"You've picked a good day," Denny remarks. "No waves, no rough weather. You should see this thing [he motions to his boat, a small white platform in a sea of blue] when it gets windy. And you should see me when there aren't any fish. It can get very depressing. That little run we just had was nice, but you shouldn't think it's a luxury. We *have* to get them like that."

In his late twenties, Denny has been fishing eight years. It has been his only job, and in the course of his career, he has owned four boats. The three forerunners of the one we are on were all smaller. Like Mack, Denny's perspective is balanced. He likes to fish, prefers it vastly over other kinds of work, but does not see it as the center of his soul: "It's good work, but let's not get carried away by it." Not a co-op member, Denny attaches symbolic significance to joining. "I could join any time, I know they would have me," he explains, "but I don't know if I'm ready to make that kind of commitment to fishing."

The biggest problem in the work, Denny thinks, is self-discipline: "Every morning you've got to make that decision about going out there. You've got to decide when it's early—so early it's dark and you're tired and maybe a little hung over. Coming out here, putting the hook in the water, pulling in the fish—they're easy, once you've got yourself up and out of bed."

JIGGING WORK

The day progresses through many bursts of travel from one "promising" fishfinder blip to another. We have no further bonanzas. By 2 P.M. we are getting reports over the CB about fog coming in at the harbor. Denny calls the pier to check, and though their report is "all clear," he is not happy. "Sometimes it takes a little while to find the channel," he explains, and we pull in our lines to head back.

When we enter the channel—after a few misses and some eerie searching in the fog, listening for the bell buoys—Denny gives me the wheel so he can do the cleaning and dressing. I offer to help with these, but he declines because he thinks we'll get back faster if he does it by himself and I keep up a good pace through the twisting channel. Besides, his allowing me to pilot the boat is a gift. The boat is for working, true, but it's still a boat, and piloting it is an adventure. He proceeds with the dressing, and in a matter of minutes, we are surrounded by squawking gulls diving for the fish entrails.

Denny's cleaning and dressing finish up, and we are left with about three hundred dollars worth of fish—not a bad day, but below average for recent weeks. He has brought in two and a half boxes, he thinks, as compared with the fourteen or fifteen boxes that Mack had brought in long-lining. As we get closer to the dock, we check our catch with that of nearby boats. One jigger has got nine boxes, another six. Both are ecstatic. A few have got only one.

Denny reminds me that he moors his boat in a cove near his house, not near the dock, so I can get off at the town pier. Despite a desperate urge to go home, Denny stops at the pier. Already, he is checking the tide schedule for tomorrow, figuring out how early he will have to go to bed tonight.

MAKING FISHING WORK: VARIATIONS

Denny, Fred, and Mack illustrate the extent to which fishing work can be made, the extent to which it can be quite different things for different people. Mack, for example, has traveled up the career ladder of the industry, progressing through increasingly larger boats and concentrating throughout on fishing as a business. Denny, on the other hand, comfortable in his hunt-and-run, high-speed, high-tech approach to jigging, is reluctant to focus on business to a point that would mean losing contact with the fish. Long-lining does not appeal to him, no matter how profitable it may be. Denny recognizes that he may change, though, and with a measure of insight predicts that if he stays in fishing for a few more years, he will probably want to give long-lining a try. Fred does not question the decision to do long-lining. He also doesn't like the approach, but he's just waiting to get enough capital to buy the bigger boat and the accessory equipment.

Actually, the choices that Denny, Mack, and Fred have made about their respective fishing strategies are interwoven with matters that extend beyond their feelings about a work experience. Mack's work at long-lining, as opposed to jigging, is in part a reflection of his personal priorities ("Anybody can stand there and jig a hook up and down," he maintains) and of the financial needs of his family. His long-standing fishing cronies—all long-liners themselves—would hoot him out of town if he went back to jigging. Nor do his family's financial needs make it possible for him to entertain a less businesslike approach to fishing.

With no wives and children making financial demands and a different set of values held by their peers, Denny and Fred take a more sporting stance. They don't much enjoy the industrial overtones of long-lining, and they have much to say about the inherent strength and beauty of their current approach to fishing. In the end, though, their relatively minimal financial necessities are what enable them to pursue fishing in the way they like.

Fishing for Mack is the meal ticket for himself, his family, his children's college, maybe a trip to Hawaii. Also, it is, through the co-op, his chief source of visibility and pride in the community of his peers. It's simply not so serious for Fred, a bachelor on the make whose roots in the town could probably be pulled up whole. And it's even less serious for Denny, who has had a hard time for the past few years deciding, at the end of the ski season, if he should move back from the mountains once again.

Fishing work can encompass and respond to the needs, interests, and priorities of as diverse a trio as Denny, Fred, and Mack. Each has found a niche within the "industry" that is right for him. The industry, however, is far more flexible and responsive to individual needs than even the diversity of Denny, Fred, and Mack suggests. Within the industry is also a large group of fisherman on the margins: part-timers, weekenders, semihobbyists. The old-timers in Barnham call them the "mosquito fleet." Despite the frailty of their equipment, they may hope to earn a substantial amount of money from their work. At the other extreme, there are long-liners who keep their boats at sea day and night, maintaining several crews and, in some cases, managing a handful of large crews.

Within all the potential diversity, Fred, Mack, and Denny are in some ways actually quite similar. During the fishing season, each works about the same number of hours and days. Each renews his commitment to the industry at about the same rate—and early in the morning, long before the first light of sunrise, each confesses, with some pride, to taking the risks inherent in spending as much time as possible at sea, going out despite ominous weather forecasts and staying out in bad conditions. Each loves the sea, the feel of fishing, the taste of fish. Each is intimately attached to his boat. At their different steps in fishing's career ladder, Denny, Fred, and Mack share a similar degree of intensity in their commitment to the work.

The source of such commitment is in the sheer power of the everyday experience of fishing. The power comes in part from the awesome beauty of the setting: the piercing colors of sunrise in a foggy, quiet harbor; the spectacle of whales frolicking off the port bow; the enormity of the sky. Some of the power of the fishing experience comes from the control of the boat: standing at the helm with feet spread apart to keep balance in a rolling sea, checking the compass against the view through a fogged windshield, feeling the engine vibrations through legs, stomach, and throat. The power of fishing comes perhaps most strongly through the hunt: tracking and finding fish, pulling them in, bringing them back to port.

The beauty, the boat, and the hunt add a dimension of macho sport to fishing work. In some ways, fishing work is based on a simple economic equation that relates income to effort. The equation is complicated, however, by the not wholly rational nature of the effort. Rewards in fishing come not only from a carefully planned expenditure of effort, but

from playing beyond one's limits. Some of the best days are
the hardest ones.

INHERENT DILEMMAS OF FISHING WORK: COSTS OF
CONTROL

Even the best days of fishing are not without troubles,
however. Fishing work involves several costs and dilemmas
that seem intrinsic, unavoidable, and, in some cases, quite
painful.

The fishermen we met like their work well enough, but
few if any of them experience the dilemma confronted by
some white-collar workers and craftsmen of finding it difficult to stop. The fishermen seem as interested as most blue-
collar workers in cutting their work time to a minimum.

Unlike most blue-collar workers, however, the fishermen
feel the pinch of reduced work effort quite directly and severely. Fishermen do control their work, but one cost of that
control is that they are placed in close contact with the vag-
aries, ambiguities, and, ultimately, the harshness of the
workplace and the marketplace. The impacts of a decision to
not go to work today may be (painfully) felt tomorrow; little
wonder, then, that tinkering with the odds of fishing production can hold such compelling interest for the fishermen.

Control has an additional, more psychological cost as
well. The ability to choose one's hours and days involves the
cost of willpower and design. There are no organizational
sanctions, no threats or punishments for staying away, but
there are no external rewards either. The only psychological
incentives for getting up and out are internal. The fishermen
enjoy exercising this will, or willpower, to a certain extent,

but they also report that it is tiring, and that it places on them a burden of responsibility that often detracts from the ex-hiliration of the work.

Once they're up and going, there is also the additional responsibility of designing and carrying out the day. The fishing workday is filled with decisions: when to leave, where to go, what to fish for, what equipment to use, how long to stay out. As with the decision to go out at all, the smaller decisions involve a burden of responsibility, and a possibly direct impact on the financial returns of the day. There are odds involved in each decision, and the ultimate unpredictability of the enterprise threatens the extent to which making any of the decisions can realistically be seen as exercising control.

Unpleasant but necessary tasks also limit the fishermen's full control of their work. They have to swab the decks, gut the fish, maintain the boats out of season. They have to keep books, pay social security, sell their fish, and make sure they haven't been cheated. If they get involved with the co-op, they can be assured of a measure of financial integrity, but then they are saddled with the responsibilities of participating in co-op governance and management. The co-op manager attributes both the strengths and the weaknesses of that organization to the members' deep-seated preference "to be alone."

The need to define fishing as "work" also extracts a price from the fishermen. They don't sit around in the local bar and hold existential debates on whether what they did that day was "work" or not, and they quite clearly distinguish themselves from the interloping sports fishermen. Yet, they are concerned about their personal image to themselves and in the community. They like to be viewed as "serious" and look to organizations like the co-op to legitimize their work as well as to improve their economic situation.

TINKERING WITH THE ODDS

For good reason, the fishermen are obsessed with production. It's a plus if the weather is good and the seas calm,
but the pressing question is always: How big is the catch?

Conflicting myths provide instruction on how to ensure
getting a big catch. One set of myths is fatalistic, maintaining
that most production is explained by fates and forces that are
always incomprehensible and unpredictable, and often per-
verse. These myths help console the hard-working fisherman
who watches his buddy, anchored a hundred yards off, pull
in six fish for every one that he himself gets.

Other myths attribute good production to perseverance:
more fish, they contend, result from more hours and more
trips. These myths help console the fishermen who take risks
on stormy and icy days to carry out their work. Still other
myths enshrine improvements in the odds, making legend
(or gossip) of eccentric, sly, or innovative techniques. The
oldster who dunks his head in the freezing water to talk with
the fish and the newcomer with the fast, new boat and expensive electronic gear are of continuing and compelling interest
to the fishermen because they threaten the balance between
fisherman and fish: they tinker with the odds.

At different times and in different ways, Mack, Fred, and
Denny have subscribed to both the fatalistic and the odds-
tinkering myths. Fred quite clearly attributes his financial
success to his willingness to take risks and go out on stormy
days. Yet, he is also attuned to new methods and equipment.
Mack claims fishing is "only a job" and doggedly maintains a
regular schedule, yet he loses all his humility when he describes his ability to find fish without electronic gear. His
innate abilities, he believes, help him tinker with the odds.

Both the fatalistic and the odds-tinkering myths are root-
ed in the fishermen's need to control. In some ways, control

is an elusive and yet obsessive theme. They must control boat, wind, weather, and, ultimately, the fish, in order to make a living. Owning a fishfinder or a bigger boat or belonging to the co-op all have the secondary impact of enhancing control, and this must be critically important among people who so highly value independence.

At the same time, control seems destined to elude the fishermen. How can they fully control their work when they must regularly trade off physical danger against financial rewards? When the market, even with the co-op helping, is nearly impossible to influence? When the fish themselves come and go unpredictably?

Chapter 3

WAYS OF POTTING

It should be obvious that what is central about the work of a potter is the pot. Even after thousands of years, the physical product that rises out of the shapeless clay via the potter's hand could still strike a poet as the metaphor for God's creation.

But what rises from the clay may be thought of in the framework of artistic creation as a work of art, or it may be thought of in a utilitarian framework as a vessel for practical use. The potter may be an artist, or a production potter. The work of potting is actually multiple, and its components are extremely diverse. There are:

Wedging and preparing clay
Designing
Shaping
Firing
Marketing
Setting up, organizing, and maintaining a studio

Each of these may be done in various ways. To change the process of wedging and preparing clay seems to require technological changes, which in turn make other demands on the process (capital investment, machinery, employees, and a market that can support these). Other choices can be made at the level of the very small or one-person firm; marketing may be done to larger distributors (e.g., Macy's) that sell a more-or-less standardized product, or via galleries which sell one-of-a-kind art objects; this choice, too, while not carrying the sorts of scale implications required by the preceding one, has further consequences, for one cannot sell to galleries without the process of keeping up contacts, which some people seem to find even more onerous than doing standardized production for the less "interesting" alternative.

One way potters derive satisfaction is by carrying out several of these functions: "A change is as good as a rest." Or functions may be specialized and embellished, with potters choosing not to change and rest.

To examine how functions of potting may be organized to yield various kinds of satisfaction, we focus on the ways potting is carried out in a cooperative studio in Cambridge, Massachusetts. Since the variation in the studio is of individual arrangements within a single work setting, we begin with shorter descriptions of some other arrangements: three different ways of framing the work of potting in one small town in Vermont.

THE SOLITARY CRAFTSPERSON

The first of these Vermont potters, a Master of Fine Arts from Bennington College, is now back in Vermont after three years largely spent sailing in her brother's boat across the

Atlantic and back. She supports herself by potting. She sells to a limited number of substantial distributors; she says that so far, she has "not had to" go around to the stores, but to expand, she would need to do so. These distributors want fairly standardized things. She is in effect a one-person production potter. For ten or eleven months a year, she works all day alone in a small shed, making mugs and bowls; as we talked, she shaped and attached handles to mugs she had thrown in the morning, about two minutes per handle, each like the last; she was at this point working from 8:30 or 9 A.M. to 11 P.M. or so to meet an order. She said that she had no desire at all to have anyone else working with her; she would find another's presence intrusive. Every year after the Christmas rush, there is slack period of a month or so during which she can—if she organizes her life in that way—do creative work. During this period, she said, she had an annual "identity crisis." She said that she would not consider spending twenty years this way but at the moment is perfectly satisfied. She looked satisfied, and although she was working away—it seemed—as fast as she could while maintaining a steady pace, there was no discernible tension in her voice or hands. She explained that with mugs, "it is in the hands," and the more you do, the better they get. A few days before, she had made sixty mugs in a day to see if she could do it; she barely made her self-imposed quota, but that day's mugs were the best of all.

The satisfaction she derives appears to be centered on independent craftsmanship—although it is an independence so sharply constrained by the economics of the business as to look like a kind of slavery. But the constraints are self-imposed.

The mugs come forth; the skill in making them and the capacity to make a living by potting are for the moment enough.

A POTTERY BUSINESS

In the same town, there is a large pottery run by a man whom we shall call Robert Jackson. He began as an individual craftsman. He started to pot in high school, went to Alfred College to learn ceramics, visited galleries, and apprenticed himself. He spent ten years experimenting with a more craftsmanlike form of production, in a barn studio in Vermont; indeed, he had planned to begin as part of a four-man collective, but the other three members dropped out. At various times, he had other people working with him. Looking back on these relationships, he sees them as ambiguous, confused, part employee, part collaborator, with Jackson always having the bottom-line responsibility for finances in the end. His current style, with "boss" and "employees" as defined and clearly separate roles, is, in part, a response to the discomforts of those ambiguities.

Twenty years ago, he bought a larger plant in the center of town. He has in the twenty years expanded on this base with the aid of loans from both the local bank and the Small Business Administration. Now, he does a million dollars worth of business in a diversified operation consisting of a number of different lines of pottery, a plant store, a children's store, and a gourmet restaurant. When he gets his tunnel kiln installed, he expects to do three million dollars worth of business a year. He has ninety employees and is currently engaged in controversy with the work force, which has been organized by the International Ladies Garment Workers Union.

Jackson has not thrown a pot for nearly a year. He does some designing, but mainly his field of creativity is the business: "It moves my head. It keeps my head turning." Locating new markets is interesting and challenging; he approaches this task with a kind of spirit of the chase. He's pleased with the designs. He does have trouble being a boss;

he is, even by local standards in a low-wage area, a conspicuously low-wage employer; he gets workers whom he doesn't always respect; he is hard with them and is uncomfortable about it. It seemed clear that he would find it uncomfortable to have me interview his workers, and the interview had to force its way past a thicket of defensiveness toward someone presumably committed to workplace democracy.

ARTIST AND EMPLOYER

One might think that Jackson's designer–model-maker would be dissatisfied by having so much of the design and initiative role in the business captured by her boss. But she also seems very satisfied with her job. She, too, started as an artist potter and studied at Alfred College, in England, and elsewhere. What she likes about her role is the freedom to take part in or look on and learn a number of complex tasks connected with potting, while at the same time keeping herself free to be an artist and a human being who is not defined by the job. She says that if she is going to do potting and sculpture she wants to do it to please herself, not to please the galleries. She finds learning about markets fascinating. She does not find the designing she does for Jackson, even though he initiates, too constraining for satisfaction, and she does her own work in the shop after hours. She says she must be one of the few people in town who gets on splendidly with her boss. For her, the "work" pottery supports the "hobby" pottery-sculpture in an agreeably balanced way.

THE POTTERY STUDIO

The Pottery Studio represents a different framing for pottery from any of those just described. It is a cooperative studio in which the members share the facilities and engage in a

great deal of personal interaction, while still working individually and dealing as individuals, even idiosyncratically,
with the place that potting plays in their lives.

The studio's founding members met in a summer pottery
course. One is a woman who had studied anthropology,
found "it turned me off," took one course in pottery, and was
"hooked immediately." The other is an architect-planner
who had begun potting as a hobby but who almost immediately began thinking, "How many cups would I have to sell
to live from this?" Neither had had a place to work; both
wanted a salt kiln, which represented more capital than either or both together could muster. They began to look for
others. By the time they found a suitable space that seemed
right, there were five in the group; when this space did not
work out, they redoubled their energies, combing the city for
a possible loft, and attaching new members. Finally, they
found a space in an old industrial building.

They settled on a size (twelve members) and a cost structure linked to the rent of the industrial loft space they have
found. Each member would advance a share of the total estimate for the initial renovation of the space, the construction
of the kiln, and the finishing of the display, kitchen, and
bathroom areas. Subsequently, each member would contribute on a monthly basis toward the rent and upkeep. The
figures were within reach of all the members and offered
them a bargain in access to space and equipment.

The quarters the group settled on provided space for the
kiln, a gallery, more than a dozen work spaces, a kitchen, a
bathroom, and storage. Accommodating all this affordably
and legally locating the kiln led the group to one of the vacant
old factories in one of the town's more disreputable neighborhoods.

On balance, the physical location is actually quite good,
convenient to public transportation, and easily located by

out-of-towners. The factory building's numerous windows afford an abundance of natural lighting, and its construction makes it possible to cluster the heavy equipment and still have a reasonably unobstructed view through the studio. Also, unlike some industrial neighborhoods, this one has a fairly high and constant volume of traffic from shoppers and workers.

Once located and agreed on, the studio demanded a tremendous amount of work. It needed painting throughout, as well as bathroom and kitchen facilities. Racks had to be built for storage, and tables constructed for working. The kiln had to be built. The twelve members of the group spent about six months working on preparing the studio for beginning use.

The early months were fraught with difficulties and frustration. The members wanted to get down to business and start potting, but the amount of preparation work was staggering. Because they wanted to save money, they did most of the work themselves, but this kept them away from potting. Also, because they were not very accomplished at the repair and renovation work they attempted, they spent more time at it than they expected and made mistakes. By the time the studio had its formal opening, the members were ecstatic to be out of the carpentry business and very ready to get on with the potting.

Because the transformation of the space was so complete and the work so extensive, the time the members put into the building process later came to take on a mythical quality. This was the time of getting started, of proving they would make a stand. The physical space visibly reflected their energies—as it was transformed from a dark, dingy, dirty factory area to a clean, aesthetic, artful artists' place.

The building period affected how the individuals were perceived and how the group as a whole was thought of. The individuals who worked at tasks that were important for the

group acquired importance. The members who had acquired
carpentry skills taught as much as they could to others but
tended to take on a central role themselves.

GROUP PROCESS

Perhaps because they couldn't make any real decisions
about operating until they had a physical site and full membership, the original members developed a good deal of sensitivity to their own processes of interaction. They spent less
time making decisions than deciding how to decide. In one
sense, they regarded these efforts as good business practice
and as laying the foundations for smoother operations to
come.

In another way, though, they also quickly recognized
that they enjoyed their sensitivity to the group's interaction.
That the group existed for over a year without actually pro-
ducing any pots was indicative not only of the constraints
they faced but also of the way they worked: putting the concerns of "the group" on a par with those of production. From
the outset, the group has often encountered the allegation,
made by members and by observers alike, that it was less
than clear if potting or the group came first.

The group's process awareness helps make its meetings
more productive. Meetings look informal. Members cluster
on the old, overstuffed sofas and chairs next to the kitchen,
sipping tea and eating brownies. There are no *Robert's Rules*.
Yet the group's meetings are also businesslike in some important ways. There are agendas and lists of topics to discuss.
The group makes decisions that are clear, and that most
members understand and commit themselves to support.
After a meeting, members seldom ask, "What did we
decide?"

These interactions are strongly colored by the involvement of many of the group's members in EST. The EST com-

mitment leads individuals to stress "responsibility" and "being up front" about feelings; it makes for a high level of energy in group interactions. The EST terminology enters into the way the members talk about even the work of potting. They talk, for example, about confronting the clay, and about the need to do the dirty work that is a part of potting, and about taking responsibility for the tedious aspects of the work that they had previously ignored. "Ever since I took the EST workshop," one of them observed, "I take extra care so the lids fit tightly on all my pots."

For the "hold outs" who have not entered the training, EST is something of a divisive issue.

The flow of interpersonal emotionality that runs through work life at the studio may be experienced as nourishment for the creative life. But it can also be a source of instability. One member described, in a moving way, how the studio was the center of her life and work. The next week, having "worked out" her feelings, she left the group for the unemployment lines. The consensus of the group was that she had never really been clear in her feelings. The clarity of the group's process apparently hadn't helped.

The group process and the nourishing interpersonal emotionality also confront some tough economic facts.

Where was the money to come from for the new kiln? And what would be done about the space left by members off on extended summer vacation or, in one case, six months in Europe? The obvious answer seemed to be to rent space to additional potters. But these people would not be part of the group, just paying tenants. What would this do to the atmosphere of the Studio?

Here are excerpts from a meeting where the issue was discussed:

D: If we are building a new kiln, this would help draw in members.

H: Why not set a goal of getting five members to make renting attractive and easy?

D: Produces calculations showing various combinations of full-time, part-time and associate members and how the finances would work out.

E: Even so, the monthly falls short of meeting the financial need.

J: For me, it isn't worth a lot more people.

D: If we're going to be twenty people, we'll have to build in enough kiln space.

E: I don't get the part time and full time—sometimes I'm very part time.

J: There have to be limitations on space and firing privileges or everyone will want to be part time.

S: It's like Radcliffe! (I.e., the impersonally run studio that several members left to form the Pottery Studio.)

H: Why not make the end of the studio into communal space for ten part-time people? We could use that space for students.

J: We could fill it temporarily and then make plans during the summer.

E: We should make the plans *with* the new people.

H: Why not do a raku workshop?

D: Maybe do one workshop every month.

J: It would be like a fucking sale every month.

H: Have fifteen people in the workshop; the studio takes a cut.

J: Fifteen people is going to feel like something. . . .

E: We need to rent, use the money to get equipment. We need to set goals, make plans.

H: It will be faster to get part-time members because they pay less.

S: The salt kiln should be reserved for members. It's so much work. *They* should fire electrically.

A: I wouldn't come into the studio with only an electric kiln.

J: We've never had *advantages* for people who pay more. We could have communal firings once a month for people who are part time.

E: I don't see them buying in as members—we're just renting space to raise money to get equipment—and to pay off Ginny, Neville, and Sue.

D: We need four eighty-dollar people by August first to be back at break-even. . . .

H: It's five times the space of the Museum School with seventy students.

J: But we paid one thousand dollars to avoid that. I need *more* space—a big table.

D: We're creating a new kind of thing. We wanted to create a space for all of us to work. Now we're creating an institution like Mudflat or Radcliffe or MIT—to make enough money for all of us to work—but in creating this new institution there is much more of a management problem.

The last speaker has summarized the problem succinctly. It seems to have no ready solution. The group was still struggling with it when we left.

POTTERY WORK

The work of potting is an artistic process and hence involves a kind of thinking and a level of emotion alien to many work experiences.

One effect of doing art as work seems, for some of the potters, to be an integration of their self-identity with their work. They see the work not merely as production but as self-expression; they invest much of themselves in the work. In an extreme instance, one member of the studio observes, "Everything that I am, I get from my work. I get all my strokes from my work." Conversely, when the work isn't going well (and the potting muse can be fickle, so this may happen frequently), the personal psychological effects can be devastating.

Self-employment of any kind demands the discipline to persist, to keep regular hours, and to work consistently, and these issues of pure endurance can be difficult in any kind of work. The potters have all these endurance issues of persistence in addition to having the slippery creative process to put into harness.

Intellectualizing aside, the production work of potting is fairly straightforward. Its basic components haven't changed much in the past several centuries. The pots start with clay:

damp, tactile, malleable. The studio buys clay in bulk, purchasing a variety of textures and colors—clays with different properties conducive to different kinds of shaping and useful for different end products.

Once the clay is chosen and mixed, it may be shaped and sculpted while stationary or while on a wheel. Most sculpted products are not utilitarian but more for decoration—abstract art pieces of straight sculpture. The wheel is the essence of most potting, for it makes it possible to produce circular objects of all kinds. The wheel also holds much of the fascination of potting production, making the clay a dynamic, moving entity that responds deftly to pushes and shoves.

After the clay has been shaped, it is left to age for a bit, is perhaps covered with a glaze, and is then put into a kiln. This aspect of potting is the most technologically difficult, because kiln temperatures must be extremely high in order to bake the clay properly. At the temperatures required, it is difficult to regulate the degree of heat accurately, and slight differences may burn, melt, or underbake the pots. After all their work on the wheel and in sculpture, the potters submit their half-finished products to a kiln that may roast them to ashes. Expensive, factory-produced kilns are more predictable but are not at all within the financial reach of even a dozen people who've pooled their resources.

The studio's kiln was regarded with awe and fear for quite some time. After several months of tenuous firings, that fear began to turn to mastery as members of the group came to learn the kiln's many eccentricities. Eventually, the group became adept at firing the kiln, and charred pots became the exception rather than the rule. Still, however, the kiln has retained some aura of mystery and eccentricity. A firing is a highly charged, dramatic event. The joy of firing the kiln is more a group experience, something that members of the studio share. Often, a firing includes the works of several people and involves all of them in the firing-up and monitoring process over a number of hours. Some of the studio's most legendary firings took place late on summer nights, ending with wee-hour unbrickings of the kiln and an impromptu celebration of success.

Once the pot has been fired, there is some controversy about where the work of the potter ends. Some say that potting begins and ends in the studio, but others feel that potters need to take an active role in selling their wares. Most potters can't afford to take the former stance; those that can tend to be fairly accomplished artists who contract to marketers or agents to sell their work for them. Even accomplished potters may choose to market their own work, though, because selling through wholesalers cuts in on a substantial proportion (often 40 percent) of the price. That 40 percent has to be made up somewhere—in reductions in the potter's returns and/or in the potter's need to increase production. Also, a number of potters enjoy the interpersonal contact of marketing because it provides "strokes," a break from the work of the studio, and some feedback with respect to the kinds of potting work people are interested in buying.

Most members of the studio enjoy some direct contact and sales work, but they are also interested in finding ways to market their pots that will enable them to spend more time in design and production. They've looked to the gallery on the premises of the studio as a vehicle for selling their work and have slowly increased the gallery's sales volume over the years. However, the studio's location is not yet well enough known to have the gallery account for significant sales, and the group has not yet put enough work into marketing the gallery to have it overcome its lack of visibility on the local arts scene.

The most notable thing about the whole work process, from clay mixing through wheel work through firing and sales, is the extent to which it is artful and emotional. Shaping a pot on the wheel conjures up strong feelings: respect for the clay, surprise at a new curve, enjoyment of a particular kind of shape.

Even sales has its artful dimensions, for example, the stories of some Studio members who, when it was their turn to man the gallery space, somehow always seemed to sell more than any four other members.

DIFFERENCES AND INDIVIDUALS

Potting work offers a number of different choices: how much to produce, when, and what. It also offers the possibility, in a number of ways, for choice in artful and creative practices: how often to fire the kiln, how seriously and intensely to market the product. However skilled they may be at clarifying and discussing their differences, the members of the studio differ widely in the choices they make about potting and the kinds of art they pursue. The differences place a continuing strain on the group.

For Dick, for example, the studio is first and foremost a convenient work space. With years of experience and success on his own, Dick's main reason for joining the studio was that it is more convenient to his home than his previous work space. He keeps conspicuously regular hours, and his area is noticeably more full of work than those around him. He's tolerant of the studio's numerous meetings but doesn't really enjoy them. For him, there is minimal art in the work; mostly, he's concerned with making a daily production quota. He doesn't wax eloquent about confronting the clay, but he does make it clear that he's very happy doing potting work, and happy to be in the studio.

Irene, on the other hand, is in it mostly for the studio and the group. Irene is not a very accomplished potter. She's in the studio to learn, to be sure to take enough time to invest in potting so she can find out how good she might become. She's saved enough money from her previous job to "buy" almost a year of "discovery time," full-time participation in the studio.

Previously a legal secretary, Irene savors the opportunity she has each morning to decide whether and when she will come in. Most often, her decision is to come, and to come early and stay late. She sees her role in the studio as a combination of mother hen, chef, confessor, and custodian. She's fully aware that the others may not need or even particularly want to take such a position. She's grateful that the group can accommodate her desire to invest so much of herself. "It's something that I want to do at this point in my life," she observed. "Two years from now I may be back in the law office, but for now, this is what I want to do."

Evelyn operates at a slower pace than Irene or Dick. She is intense and reflective, and her contributions to group discussions are few but well respected by the other members of the group. It's as if she continuously weighs the tenor of the discussion, then sums it up for the group, adding her own observations and suggestions. Often, her contributions to group discussions are "stoppers" that have the quality of pronouncements. In many cases, Evelyn is the decider, and she knows it.

Evelyn's potting, too, is careful and intense. Her designs are innovative, but always with a sense of flow and grace. She shies away from tricks and gimmicky products, concentrating mostly on traditional pots—but always with an air of elegance that sets them apart.

Despite her talents and skill in the craft, Evelyn maintains a continuing debate with herself regarding her continuation in the studio. She hasn't really convinced herself that she is a potter. She sees the meetings drudgery and obligation, but she seems to use them to elicit support from other members of the studio in the definition of her career.

The other members of the group vary similarly in their views on meetings, obligations to the group, ability in the craft, self-discipline, production output, sales volume, and expectations of the studio. All of members' feelings also change and shift. Sometimes, there seems to be a unity of feelings, and when the unity is around enthusiasm, the contagion is noticeable and positive. On the other hand, there have also been downward swings of group emotion that have practically leveled the studio. After the Christmas holidays one year, the predictable emotional drop was compounded by troubles with the kiln and the departure of several of the studio's members. Everyone's production dropped. For some, it stopped completely. The physical trappings of the studio went to seed. The gallery accumulated dust; the plants died. The stove broke, and water for coffee had to be heated in the broiler or the oven.

On balance, though, the snowballing of members' sentiment is less frequently a problem than the need of the studio to respond to the diverse demands and expectations that members have. However it may affect production, the studio's skills with the group process help it respond to these demands.

A Morning in the Pottery Studio

The morning we are describing presents an abnormal task: the rebuilding of the kiln. The original kiln, the piece of capital equipment that was, in a practical sense, the *raison d'être* of the enterprise, proved defective. Now, the potters are having, slowly, with difficulty, and expensively, to make a new one. The building of the kiln is an additional task, and also the reason for a certain loss of energy; it is as if the fire has gone out in the room. In this respect, the situation may be said to be abnormal.

But it is not wholly so. People can still pot; when they need to fire, they use the kiln belonging to the pottery cooperative on the floor below. The pieces of work are not discontinuous with "ordinary times."

At 9:30 A.M., the studio seems very quiet. The racks of unfired pots, the unpainted floor, make a quiet pattern of grays and buff. Two people are in the studio. Sarah is making coffee and offers me a cup. Don is in the "living-room area"—a couple of old couches and a beat-up coffee table—working on the accounts with a small calculator. There is a leisurely discussion between the two as to when the chimney for the kiln will come. It definitely will not come today. Sarah decides to break up old brick for kiln insulation. I join her in this, both of us wearing masks and kerchiefs. After a while, Sarah asks Don if we could have some music. He says, "Do you really want it?" Detecting negative reaction, Sarah asks if he minds. He says no and turns on the radio.

At one point, Sarah tears off her mask to express indignation about a radio commercial stating that aspirin wards off heart attacks; people shouldn't be encouraged to take so many drugs. At 10:40, Miranda, the apprentice, arrives, puts on an apron, and starts getting ready to work.

Shortly after this, a woman arrives looking for Evelyn, who it seems she is expecting to teach a class. Those in the studio point out the sign saying that the class will be on Tuesday. The woman says she yelled at the baby-sitter for coming late; she can't come tomorrow. She repeats several times, "She didn't call me."

Sharon, another potter, arrives. She discusses with Miranda a haircut she had given her, which they agree should be shorter in front. Sharon agrees to cut it some more.

Miranda tells Sarah that one of the lights is out. They fix

it together, meanwhile discussing the antinuclear demonstration in Washington that Sarah has attended.

Don has moved over to the big table to work on the accounts. It's a complicated job, he tells me: Some things are assessed in advance, and some things delivered have not yet been assessed. Each individual has his or her own account.

By 11, Miranda is working away steadily, making mugs.

There is a discussion of the Pottery Studio business card. At a meeting of the cooperative, there was a vote to have a new card that, instead of saying "a pottery cooperative," refers to "pottery and sculpture" and a "gallery." Sarah is very bothered by the elimination of the words "a pottery cooperative." "That's why I'm here," she says. Sharon explains that the reasoning was that *cooperative* has to do with their internal organization, and that *pottery*, *sculpture*, and *gallery* relate to "outside." At the meeting, Jill, who most wanted the change, and whose pottery is most in the "galery" mode, had said that "a pottery cooperative sounds like sixties organic." The upshot of all this discussion is a decision to get some of the old cards "in the meantime."

Bob, another member of the studio, arrives wearing a straw hat. There is a discussion of the recent yard sale to raise money for the kiln. Bob has been driving around in a truck trying to dispose of things left over from the sale. Sharon tells Bob about the decision on the cards. He agrees. Miranda is potting steadily away.

Sharon calls the materials supplier. She reports that the next load of bricks will arrive tomorrow between 10 and 11.

Bob says, "I have a lot of yard work to do. I might as well do it. Dan and I are signed up for tomorrow. It took a long time to get that stuff to the place."

Sharon says, "That's working too."

Sarah is looking at a plant. She says it needs repotting:

"There's always something to keep me from doing what I ought to do."

Bob makes a telephone call to get a profit-and-loss statement he needs for the accounts.

Now up from the table, Bob goes over and admires the mug Miranda has just made. Miranda says she needs to make a thousand like it. Sharon, also, is now admiring the pot. Sharon says that making a thousand is just like making one; even if it's a thousand it's still one at a time.

Ann, another of the group, arrives and is greeted. She says she is meeting a friend, will have lunch at Erewhon (an organic restaurant), and be back at 1:30 to work: "I'll do *anything.*"

There is a discussion of whether the kiln should have peepholes.

    Ann: It looks *fantastic.*
Sharon: From now on, it's all downhill.
    Sarah: That's a *beschrei.*

This sets off a discussion of wonderful Yiddish all-encompassing words.

Sharon starts wedging clay.

Sarah notices that the paste-ups for the cards and posters are still by the table and asks Sharon, "Do you want to put this back or have me do it?" Sharon says she's "into clay" and that Sarah could do it.

Bob notes Miranda looking at her output and says, "You can think about them, why this one came out taller and so on." Miranda: "I'm not really into that at this point." Bob: "Well, you can when you feel like it."

At this point a man arrives wearing a business suit and carrying a briefcase. Sharon goes to deal with him and gives him the old card.

Sarah and Bob tell Ann about their decision on the card.

Sarah, Bob, and Ann now discuss at some length how to do the mortar for the firebox in the afternoon.

Joan, another member, appears and is greeted by Miranda.

Just before 12, Sarah starts wedging clay.

Sharon, Joan, and Miranda are now in the lounge area. Sharon cuts a grapefruit and offers me half. I decline, so she gives it to Joan, who accepts it. They are discussing the demonstration. Sarah thinks Dick Gregory's project of fasting is silly, but she is very enthusiastic about the demonstration.

Sarah asks me about the study. I explain it as a study of work. What is work? Sharon: "Work is something to do. Something to do to make money." I ask her whether making money helps or takes away from the experience. Don: "Money makes it complete." Sharon, somewhat more vaguely: "The money makes it more interesting."

In this two and a half hours, an extraordinary range of activities has taken place or has been touched on. There are: planning work on the kiln, breaking brick to make materials for the kiln project wedging clay, making mugs, and negotiating with a materials supplier.

There is also a discussion on the content of a business card, which effectively reverses the decision made in a group meeting, since the member who had felt most strongly about changing the card is now absent, and in the studio environment, the woman who wants to keep it unchanged takes a more aggressive role.

There are: doing of accounts, negotiating with the printer, a yard sale, and cleaning up after the yard sale.

There are: making coffee, repotting a plant, serving grapefruit, and the repair of a broken light.

There is also a lot of talk, only some of which is about pottery or studio business. When Sarah and Don discuss the building of the kiln, or when the group discusses the form of a business card, this is clearly part of "work." When Bob suggests that Miranda "think about" her mugs, he is clearly trying to provide some of the supervision due an apprentice. There is another set of comments that has to do with mutual reassurance in the work setting. When Sharon tells Bob that getting rid of the leftovers from the yard sale is "working too," or when Ann says that the kiln "looks *fantastic*" each is keeping the others anchored psychologically to the group and its collective enterprise. But is this not also true of the haircut and the discussion of the demonstration? Certainly, for the more political Sarah, the responsiveness of the others to her interest in the antinuclear movement is part of the way in which the studio serves her as a potter and keeps her potting.

It should be clear from the sample of behavior just described that potting at the Pottery Studio is not at all framed as work by hours of activity or rules of relevance. Indeed, the absence of specific hours or specified activities is part of what makes the studio function as it does.

The variety of activities serves as recreation from the concentrated activity of potting. Wedging clay is hard work but different work from throwing mugs; one can make one's own rhythm of alternation. Ann said in an interview, "There are mornings when I don't feel like doing my own work; then, I do the work of the studio."

The loose style of personal interaction, the moving around, and the chatting make it possible for a group of people who have so far avoided criticizing each other's work (note how cautious Bob is in dealing with the apprentice, whom it is his obligation to "teach") still to learn from each other. One of the potters who has been doing a good deal of innovating, both technically and stylistically, said in an interview, "People's work has dramatically improved. . . . People who see me do what I do get turned on to doing their work more." The mixture of interactions itself creates a special kind of work environment. One of the potters said in an interview, "It nourishes me. . . . Pottery is an emotional outlet. Work with clay is based on emotion. When I can let go, I get child-like. . . . I have an intuitive knowledge." For her, all work is assessed in terms of how it "nourishes," and the studio is nourishing: "The studio is beginning to be a really powerful, powerful place." Sharon says, "Some people really make a difference. . . . People get life from these people."

Not all members of the collective have quite this "emotional" approach to potting or to life. Some treat potting much more as a professional skill. But the role of the studio as a sensuous, emotionally suffused working environment seems to be useful to all of its members. To produce this kind of environment, it is necessary to have the workplace and work time full of elements that would not ordinarily be thought of as work-related: the smell of coffee, music on the radio, talk of haircuts and politics, potting plants, verbal stroking. The role that the EST experience plays in the group has to be understood in this context.

On the issue of pay, there are both difference and ambivalence among the members of the Pottery Studio. The feeling that "money makes it complete" or at least "more interesting," as in the discussion quoted, would bring general assent.

But at the time of our study, only four of the dozen members of the collective were supporting themselves entirely by potting, and there is a considerable range of views as to the importance of commercial success.

Helga is a serious professional potter who has long made a living by making and teaching pottery, and she shapes her activities so as to make it possible to support herself by them.

Jill thinks of herself as an artist. Her work life is punctuated by shows; she would like to sell, but showing the work is primary. Another member of the group says of Jill, "She has the idea that she's the artist and we're the mud people."

Joan had been a high school teacher who felt that "academic stuff" just "wasn't me." She decided "to switch to clay." She is not making a living at it, and not trying to: "I'm not even interested in functional stuff—it's not where it is for me." She can live on six hours a week work in high school equivalency teaching and put her emotional energy into potting.

Richard, one of the founders of the group, notes that "Artists are the only workers who support their work by doing other things." He says, "I'm interested in making art more like other professions. Selling can be just as creative." In a discussion with the others in which someone referred to the studio not wholly in joke as a "nice clubhouse," he said,

> The question is whether this is going to be a ceramics club or a pottery business. Most of us would like to make a living selling pots and spend more time here. . . . Because we're the sort of people we are we can do what other groups don't do. . . . If we borrowed twenty-five thousand dollars, we could take out ads in the *New Yorker* and market products as if they were like Steuben glass—create an image for our work. . . . Some people are satisfied doing production stuff . . . but maybe we could sell a different quality of production mugs. . . . [People] could learn that having our mugs is like having paintings.

But Richard is not himself living by selling pottery; he supports himself by work as an architect-planner. And while he says that "If I offer my work for sale, and the person turns it down, I feel as if it's not validated," he admits that if they buy it, he feels bad about having his work in the possession of people who may not properly appreciate it.

CONCLUSION AND ANALYSIS

Since the members of the Pottery Studio are divided and ambivalent about the degree to which their work as potters should be responsive to the tastes of buyers, and since, indeed, they no doubt vary considerably in their capacity to make a living from potting, to frame the work around money earnings would be deeply disturbing.

Similar considerations apply to a framing around skills and output. People vary in their skills; and they vary in their commitment to production. For the group to hold together, these differences must not become divisive. From time to time, it is said in the group that "We should criticize each other's work more," but in the same breath, it is recognized that the absence of this kind of mutual criticism prevents the laceration of social bonds, fused in parallel work activity, and in the sharing of the kitchen, which make it possible for the group to continue collaboration.

Thus, the place, the studio itself, becomes loaded with meaning.

The creation of the studio constitutes a kind of mythic charter for the whole studio enterprise. People like to talk about how Sharon and Richard started looking for a space, how they thought they had one, how it fell through, how this merely heightened determination, so that the nuclear group searched through the city sector by sector, how they found this space, how dirty it was, how they scraped the soot in masks and rebuilt. To some degree, the rebuilding of the kiln reactivated the early history.

The studio means, of course, different things to different people, but it has a shared meaning as their collective creation, the place they made out of a dirty loft, and the place where they interact as a group. This shared experience of the studio bridges their individual differences. This is one implicit reason that it is difficult for the members to rent out space to other potters; these nonparticipants in the special experience violate the specialness of the place.

The fact that the studio is such a "powerful, powerful place" may be looked at in several ways.

Its power may be the outcome of the passionate activities that have taken place: there is the creation of the studio out of raw and dirty industrial space, and the interlacing of activities that take place there now—art, and production for sale, and feeling, and eating, and argument. Or this loading of meaning on the space might be thought of as the role the place plays in the activity of potting for the members of the studio. The studio has the power to frame the activity of potting as a serious business. When people enter the studio to pot, they enter an environment that makes potting a serious business; it must be serious because the studio is a serious creation, and it was created by and for potting. The place is thus the dominant frame for the potters of the studio.

The studio was shaped out of a filthy loft as a means: a place to make pots, and to fire the pots when made. But it has become such a "powerful place" in its own right that members of the studio may spend time there not so much working as being part of the atmosphere—although this may be a way of leading up to the work of potting. But the activity of potting is also something that is chosen for its own satisfactions, rather than as a means. As Richard says, "Artists are the only workers who support their work by doing other things." So, in the world of the Pottery Studio, the relationships between means and ends, the line between vocation and avocation, which we think of as normal, are differently structured around a view of personal creativity as its own end.

Chapter 4

TEACHING
Work in a Teacher-Controlled School

Teaching is a curious kind of work. It takes, we all know, no more than two people to constitute the teaching situation, and the setting may be as simple as a log with one of the two people at each end; but it is usually practiced in large institutional settings. Teaching as a subject of thought may be engaged on many levels, from the philosophical ideas of John Dewey to the ideas of the young women of definite but modest intellectual and social aspirations who have traditionally been the teachers of the United States. The teacher in her classroom is at the bottom of a large bureaucracy, and every citizen has something to say about schools; but most of the time, the teacher works without any direct supervision.

The following pages on the making of teaching work in a teacher-controlled school are arranged in three parts. First, we make some brief comments on teaching as a profession. Second, we give a history of a teacher-run "alternative school" in Massachusetts, focusing on the meaning of teacher control in this setting. Finally, we look at a working day in the life of one very highly skilled teacher in this school, and we speculate a little on what such a working life means at the personal level.

The setting is a small town that we are calling Barton, a roughly forty-minute commute from the center of Boston. Its population is largely middle to upper-middle class, well-educated, nearly all white. There is little industry in the town itself. Many persons work in the computer and electronics industry of the outer-ring Boston suburbs. The town grew in population in the early 1960s and, as our story opens, tended to draw a distinction between a somewhat conservative set of old residents and a more politically liberal set of newcomers.

THE TEACHING PROFESSION

A major criterion for distinguishing a profession from any ordinary occupation is that in a profession, the standards and methods for carrying out the activity in question are set by the members of the profession themselves. It is the professionals who control—or, at least, who should be able to control—the nature of their work. It is this control over work standards that legitimizes the profession's control of entry into it; the professionals are those who know what properly professional work is and, therefore, those who are capable of determining who can do such work and who cannot.

Teaching has a whole professional apparatus of schools of education, professional journals, professional societies, and professional meetings that operates to discuss and define proper professional practice.

It has also come about that the activity of teaching in an

accredited (and therefore accrediting) school is largely reserved to persons who have undergone a process of professional socialization by professional educators. Teaching is
therefore a profession in the way that that term is usually
understood: an occupation, the entry into which and standards of practice for which are controlled by the members of
the occupation itself.

One would suppose, furthermore, that the organization
of the school must give the teacher a very large measure of
control over the work situation and its content. Each teacher
typically works unmonitored by other teachers, in a closed
classroom outside the view— and to a large degree, outside
the effective span of control—of the school administrator.
Teachers work with one group of children from September to
June, and thus have the potential for indoctrinating and so-
cializing their flocks to the practices they see as desirable.
Objective measures of teaching effectiveness by which outsiders might call a teacher's performance to account are conspicuously lacking.

Yet, if we compare the work situation of the teacher with
that of the doctor, we see that the teaching profession generally—and the teacher as an individual—has much less capacity than the medical professionals to set the terms of reference
for good professional practice.

Boards of education are not usually dominated by professional educators, nor is it thought proper for them to be so.
The "community" is thought to be in a very basic sense the
final arbiter of proper teaching practice at a given place and
time. Americans believe that teaching should serve the political and social values of the local community, as well as im-
parting the kinds of skills particularly appropriate to young
people coming from that community.

The teacher, although working alone, is subject to rules

of practice and to definitions of proper conduct that come from the exterior social environment, mediated through the school administrator, and, in addition, from rules of practice set by the principal himself. Children have relatively little direct authority in the classroom setting, but their parents may come in to demand or complain and, depending on the school's social placement, to have their wishes and complaints taken very seriously. Moreover, while many medical procedures can be carried out in the absence of any direct collaboration by the patient (the doctor, indeed, may be better off if the patient is anesthetized), in the classroom the teacher must motivate, reward, and stimulate children to carry out mental activities that they can easily withhold. Teachers have low social status relative to doctors; their expertise is easily questioned. Especially is this true in the primary grades, where it may appear that the work of a teacher is not all that different from what "any mother can do."

Thus, it turns out that the ordinary teacher works without the direct emotional and intellectual support of colleagues, to simultaneously control and lead a roomful of persons with sharply differing interests—to whom the teacher's relationship can easily become adversarial—to perform tasks the nature of which has been set by others, mostly other people who do not share with the teacher the experience of the classroom.

A TEACHER-CONTROLLED SCHOOL

The Model School in Barton was designed from the outset to be controlled by the teachers. The assistant superintendent, who was largely responsible for getting the school started, wanted, according to an informant who worked with him closely in the early days, to "give the teacher total power."[1] He hired the first small nucleus of teachers from the Barton system, but after this, the teachers as a group did the hiring. The town's school committee decided that the school must have a principal, but as the school took shape over an organizing summer, it was the teachers who were there first. Instead of the usual system, in which the principal hires the teachers, here it was the teachers who hired the principal, the last staff member to be selected. For the first five years at least, the principal was less a maker of policy and rules of practice for the teachers than a buffer between the teachers and the outside and, less importantly, an internal administrator.

But the power of the teachers in the Model School was never other than delegated power. The school was not initiated by teachers; it was initiated by the Barton public school system, responding to the demand from a number of parents for a new kind of public school education. All over the United States in the 1960s, there were movements for educational reform, and school systems in many towns and cities responded by setting up "alternative schools" embodying one or another vision of progressive educational reform. The Model School was one of these alternatives.

In the latter half of the 1960s, some citizens of Barton plus some members of the Barton school committee began a process of modernization. They reorganized the primary schools into a kindergarten through sixth grade structure, arranged to build a new primary school, and brought in a new change-oriented assistant superintendent. In 1970, the rather conservative superinentendent resigned, and in the following year, the change-oriented assistant superintendent became acting superintendent and put forward the idea of an

---

[1]Interview, April 25, 1969, Director of volunteer program. (*Note:* All interviews on file with Lisa Peattie.)

alternative school focused on the educational ideas of an educational consultant named Gattegno, whose ideas he had
found impressive: "Parents' dissatisfaction with the elementary schools is channeled into group meetings. There is an
uncertainty about how many people are dissatisfied and with
what."[2] In March of 1971, the school committee met "and
decided to implement the concept of the pilot school, which
will be as large as needed to accommodate interested parents.
Parents immediately began to enroll their children; over 500
entered grades 1–6 in the fall."[3]

The Model School's creation "became a highly controversial issue, splitting the town along its liberal/conservative
lines."[4] Even "throughout the first year, the school's existence was very uncertain. Reports of uncontrolled student
behavior circulated throughout the town. During the spring,
a new, more conservative school committee was elected, and
the staff felt that the school was in jeopardy."[5] The atmosphere of controversy seems to have contributed to a sense in
the school of being an in-group, and of being involved in a
very special enterprise.

The school was made possible both by the intellectual
climate of the 1960s and by the particular situation in Barton
at the time. With enrollments rising and a new school being
built, the Model School was not taking anything away from
anyone. Most children in Barton were bused to school any-
how; the parents selected which school they wanted; no parents had to send their child to the Model School unless they
so chose.

The power of the teachers in the school was always, from

[2]From an unpublished chronology of the school issued in 1978.
[3]Ibid.
[4]Mark L. Kaufman "The Model School: A Case Study," unpublished paper,
January 1977.
[5]Ibid.

the beginning, moderated by the role of the parents. The parents were not only crucial in initiating the school; they were to have a continuing role in it. The plan was to have "a school that would be part of parents' lives."[6] An elaborate program was developed for mobilizing and using parents in the school as "school volunteers," and for exploiting the special skills and information that the parents might have that would supplement that of the teachers.

The parents also serve as a pressure group for the school vis-à-vis the school committee, for example, in trying to get a new third-grade class placed in the Model School rather than in another school.

Although the assistant superintendent who was largely responsible for getting the school started wanted to "give the teachers total power,"[7] he made another programmatic commitment, besides the close relationship to parents, that was to govern teaching practice and the general operations of the school in a very basic way. This was a commitment to giving a major role in the school to the educational ideas and practices of Dr. Gattegno and his consulting firm, Educational Solutions.

This commitment was to affect classroom practice in a number of ways, both direct and indirect.

In the first place, Gattegno had developed some particular techniques—"words in color" and "algebricks"—for teaching reading and mathematics that were to be installed as the approved way of teaching these skills in the school.

In the second place, Gattegno and his group had developed an educational philosophy, referred to as *subordination of teaching to learning*, that was presented in the formative years of the school as the model of thought about educational

[6]Interview April 25, 1969.
[7]Ibid.

practice: "Our job as teachers is to help the students learn how to learn, to use what they know, and to learn from and with them as carefully and clearly as possible. Our job is not to dispense knowledge, facts, right answers, and value judgments as first priority."[8] Another Gattegno slogan ("When you know a little, you know a lot.") meant to the principal "that we try to make our experiences with students as efficient for the students as possible by building on what they already know, by trying to eliminate redundant methods and materials, and by expecting as much as possible."[9] The students were expected to develop positive reinforcement for learning from the activity of learning itself and from the confirmation of success by the teacher, rather than from treats, personalized praise, and other extrinsic rewards. The teachers were, equally, expected to be rewarded by their own experience of doing good work. In practice, this seems to have meant that the vitality of the classroom would flow not directly from teacher's charisma and energy, but from well-programmed educational materials and the learning experiences that these would present for children.

In the third place, the special relationship with Gattegno and Educational Solutions meant that funds that would otherwise have been spent for specialist teachers—in art, science, and physical education—were spent for learning workshops in words in color, Gattegno math, the subordination of teaching to learning, and other in-service training from Gattegno's group. One consequence of this direction of funds was a good deal of conflict with the school parents, who felt that their children were missing the special experiences and skills that the specialists gave in other schools. In this conflict, the parents eventually won, and they succeeded in shifting

---

[8]"Progress Report: 1977," unpublished, Fall 1977.
[9]Ibid.

funds from the consultants to a more conventional group of specialists.

A fourth consequence was conflict within the teacher group between the majority, who were happy with the Gattegno materials and relationship, and a minority, who were much less so. This conflict aroused tremendous passion and was very divisive during the early years of the school.

The fifth consequence, perhaps at a basic level that was most consequential of all, was that the teachers had to "do everything," rather than being able to shift the teaching responsibility from time to time to some special subject teacher.

A final consequence was that despite the conflicts among the teachers over the Gattegno commitment, in some ways a greater sense of solidarity among the teachers. This developed because the staff were all classroom teachers, not specialists with the special interests of specialists. Later on, when the policy changed, the teachers who saw the specialists leave a meeting on an issue that they said was "not their business" saw that the lack of specialists was one of the factors in the solidarity of the early years.[10]

The hiring process with which the school began was in itself energizing and solidarity-creating:

> All staff members participated in each interview. The dialogue was extensive. The candidates were asked what they could bring to the school vis-à-vis experience, philosophy, and talents beyond teaching. The staff members shared their views on what a school should be. At the close of each interview, the staff discussed their reactions and the impressions made by each candidate. Outstanding candidates were unanimously accepted on the spot. Sometimes, we sent observers to watch candidates in action at their own places of work.
>
> As the staff grew [it seemed] expedient to separate

[10]Interview with principal, April 24, 1969.

into smaller interviewing groups. [The teachers] expected that a large group of interviewers must be quite
awesome to the interviewees. The candidates moved
through each small group until all the staff had had an
opportunity to indulge in a dialogue with each. The candidates were finally thanked and dismissed. The staff
then reassembled to discuss their reactions and to vote
on the acceptance or rejection or 'hold' of each person
interviewed. It is interesting to note that . . . final the
decisions on virtually all the candidates were un-
animous.[11]

In view of the subsequent evolution of the school, it
seems appropriate to note here that the selection of the teachers, at the outset and subsequently, was only in exceptional
cases on the basis of observing the teacher in the classroom.
In general, the teachers were evaluated on the basis of interpersonal discussion as congenial colleagues.

The opening of the school was tremendously exciting,
and somewhat chaotic; there was a huge sense of energy
among the teachers. The building in which the school was to
be housed was one of the older and more dilapidated in the
system. Not all the materials were in place. The teachers individually organized and decorated their classrooms; hammers
and paints were brought in. There was a certain tendency for
each teacher to try to make his or her mark, in some instances, rather splashily; a sixth-grade teacher painted each
wall of his classroom in a different bright color (purple, pink,
etc.) and had a chicken coop in one corner. At one point, the
Barton Fire Department came with a truck and cleared the
building of items thought to constitute fire hazards—rugs, a
parachute for a ceiling, and so forth.[12]

A participant in this phase remarked, acutely, that "Par-

---

[11]"Hiring Procedures," undated document.
[12]Interview, April 25, 1969.

ents were upset but unable to deal with their upset; they wanted to be 'with it.' "[13] After all, they had bought into an "alternative school." And there was no consensus on how to judge the school; some parents, even at the beginning, saw the school as too traditional.

Meanwhile, the processes of self-governance in this novel teacher-run school were in themselves energizing and energy-consuming:

> During the first two years of the school . . . there was a tremendous amount of energy and activity. Teachers, students, and parents could be found in school from early morning to late night, seven days a week. Staff meetings and discussions were held weekly and attendance was mandatory. All issues, concerns, and decisions were presented to the full staff for consideration and resolution.[14]

Another participant in these early days summed it up: "It was a peak experience."[15]

In summary, teacher control turned out to mean a life of endless meetings, both exhilirating and debilitating.

Some of these meetings simply dealt with the load of decisions to be made in starting up a new, innovative institution. The principal was not inclined to take a particularly active role in the internal policy of the school; he had been hired by the teachers and "deliberately tried to maintain a neutral position."[16] Furthermore, there was plenty for the principal to do in dealing on behalf of the school with the outside world of parents, school committee, and public school administration.

But there were also internal conflicts among the staff, the

[13]Ibid.
[14]Kaufman, op. cit.
[15]Interview, April 15, 1969.
[16]Kaufman, op. cit.

negotiation of which was costly in emotional energy. Teacher
control could mean that the individual teacher practiced as he
or she saw fit within the classroom. Or it could mean that the
teachers, collectively and with some degree of unanimity,
made policy for the school and each other. In practice, it
could not wholly mean both. Early on, the teachers agreed on
a policy of unanimity, or consensus, rather than majority
rule; on "an important question," any one of them might
block a decision until agreement was reached. An "important
question" was never called, but this view of decision making
by consensus meant that all consequential issues, such as the
differences in opinion on the role of Dr. Gattegno and his
teaching methods, had to be struggled over at length:

> An extensive series of meetings was devoted to the
> creation and implementation of a "self-evaluation" pro-
> gram. In principle, this was a plan committed to teacher
> development and continuing personal and educational
> growth. It involved staff members' visiting and observ-
> ing each other and discussing their observations, and
> each individual's writing his or her own self-evaluation.
> These reports would then be presented to the full staff,
> where they would be discussed and suggestions would
> be made.[17]

Those who took part in this process agree that it was all
extremely painful. To invade the classroom territory of a fellow teacher—or worse, to have one's own classroom in-
spected and evaluated by a fellow teacher—struck at the
teacher's sense of professional autonomy where it lay closest
to the bone. During this period, some teachers decided that
work in the Model School was not for them and decided to
resign. A real difficulty was presented by a second-grade
teacher whose educational philosophy and practice of teaching clearly differed from that of his colleagues; in a differently

[17]Ibid.

organized school, such a teacher might have been urged to look for a transfer, but here, the unanimity principle made this impossible. Finally, the informal social pressure became too much and he left.

The teachers came together during the first year to defend one of their number whose tenure was threatened from outside. The assistant superintendent who had, in effect, founded the school on the basis of Gattegno's educational ideas questioned whether a teacher who had been unwilling to participate in the Gattegno summer workshops should continue teaching at the school. Even though the teachers were themselves divided on Gattegno, they found unanimity in resisting the claims of any outside administrator to intervene within the school; the teacher in question continued at the school.

In the second year, "many teachers felt that the evaluation of the first year had been destructive, and so an *ad hoc* committee began to restructure the procedure. Although the work was completed, a staff evaluation never took place during that year."[18] In the third year, the school hired a number of staff assistants to free up the teachers' time to visit each other's classrooms, so as to facilitate the mutual evaluation process. In fact, as it worked out, these staff assistants were used as supplements for classroom activities, and for a third year, the staff evaluation never took place. By 1975, after the staff had been unable to complete an evaluation for the third consecutive year, the responsibility was delegated to the principal.

In retrospect, it is hard to know how many of the difficulties of this particular version of "teacher control" were due to irreconcilable differences in ideas of education, and how much to the teachers' defensiveness of the classroom bound-

[18]Ibid

ary and of the teacher's autonomy within it. In support of the
first interpretation, it must be noted that the conflict between
the pro-Gattegno and anti-Gattegno factions continued
through these early years; a direct conflict was prevented
only by the threat of the stalemate that would be produced if
one side or the other called an "important question." The
issue disappeared only in 1975, when the teachers yielded to
parental pressure for specialist teachers in art, music, and the
like and substituted these for Gattegno in the budget. Taking
the other view, the same staff member who experienced the
early days as a "peak experience" felt that the difficulties
with evaluation were "deep down an avoidance—they
couldn't handle it."[19] Another teacher characterized the
school as "not unified, though it once was—and less then
most public schools. People work out their own solutions."[20]
Still another teacher, noting that she had never visited another teacher's classroom, said that it was only by car-pooling
that she found out what her colleagues were doing. Or the
humanities specialist might carry a report to one teacher of
what a teacher previously visited was up to.[21] Still another
teacher pointed out that "There is no built-in time to learn
here" and that the prevailing culture of the school made it
hard to ask questions of other teachers: "There was a time
when it wasn't easy to say the workshop was not helpful or to
say they needed help. Other people were dying but didn't
show it. It seemed to you everyone else was full of confidence. [You] thought if you were having trouble, you must
just need to try harder."[22]

So teacher control at the Model School has come to mean

[19]Interview, April 25, 1969.
[20]Interview, April 19, 1969.
[21]Interview, July 23, 1969.
[22]Interview, July 23, 1969.

a sort of institutional control that stops at the closed door of the individual classroom.

Meanwhile, the school was gradually becoming less controversial. During its second year, the Boston College Testing Bureau carried out a formal evaluation of all the Barton elementary schools that showed that the Model School children scored as well as or better in reading and mathematics than children in other schools. These results served to defuse a good deal of anxiety of parents about practice in the school.

In 1973, the assistant superintendent who had largely been responsible for initiating the school resigned. (He left professional education altogether and is now a builder in western Massachusetts.) Shortly after that, the superintendent, who had been new to both Barton and the job, resigned and was replaced by the high school principal, a long-term Barton resident. For the new superintendent, the Model School was less a special experiment than one of a number of schools in the system. The hiring of the subject-matter specialists took some of the parental heat off. By the time we came to the school, its teachers and principal were beginning to worry less about being exploratory and innovative, and more about how to keep up enrollments—and therefore desirability in the community—as the number of primary-school-age children dwindled, and the social movements for "alternative education" began to go out of style.

As time went by, there were more and more people working in the school who did not share the experience of the early founding years. The first replacements, who came into school in the second year of its existence, were hired through the same grueling group-interview process as the original teaching staff:

> The hiring procedures underwent a dramatic change during the summer of 1974. Three staff members, two teachers, and a counselor resigned after the close of

school. Those teachers who were available screened the applicants and selected several candidates. Since both teaching positions were part of team-teaching assignments, the final decision was left up to the other members of the team. For the counseling job, a group recommended a male social worker who was not certified as a school guidance counselor. He was rejected by the Pupil Personnel Services Department, and, for the first time, the Model School was unable to hire the candidate of its choice. When school began in September 1974, there were three new staff members who were unknown to the majority of the teachers. By the fourth year, nearly half the staff had been hired since the second year of the school.[23]

In any case, as the Gattegno counsultants reduced their role in the school, no substitute mechanism was developed to instruct teachers in the standards and practices expected of them. Indeed, no such consensual expectations existed. New teachers picked up information from one or another colleague with whom they had a personal or professional relationship, or they worked it out on their own. The specialists had different backgrounds and different roles in the school from the classroom teachers and saw their interests as different from those of the latter.

The level of group meetings at the very beginning was, of course extraordinary; but it apparently continued at a rather high level throughout the first four years. During the second year of the school's existence, three standing committees—on administration and budget, curriculum development, and facilities and materials—were organized to facilitate decision making. But these had no delegated decision-making power; they brought informational findings to the full staff, and in addition to serving on a committee, each staff member was expected to attend weekly meetings. In the third

[23]Kaufman, op. cit.

year, committees were organized around curriculum areas, and an administrative committee was formed to prepare the budget and to create agendas for large staff meetings; "however, the work of each committee, especially the administrative committee, was constantly reviewed and redone at large staff meetings."[24] During the fourth year,

> New committees were formed, including one on parent participation and involvement. The full staff met biweekly in a continuing effort to govern the school. However, teachers began to question their roles and the expectations placed upon them. Almost half the staff had been hired since the second year of the school, and it was no longer clear why the school was operating by its original design.[25]

The upshot of this discontent was a process of examination leading to a series of "organizational development" days held in May 1975. During these days, there was a far-ranging discussion of the use of time, of priorities, of working roles and conditions: "These meetings provided the first legitimate opportunity for teachers to question the amount of time they spent at school."[26] A task force worked during the summer to draft recommendations based on these discussions. When these recommendations were brought before the faculty in the fall of 1975, they were overwhelmingly accepted. Its plan "called for an end to the important question [i.e., unanimity–consensual decision-making] of abolition of mandatory attendance and quorum at staff meetings, and discontinuing decision making at large faculty meetings. . . . The full staff would meet only to review and update policies and priorities."[27]

[24]Ibid.
[25]Ibid.
[26]Ibid.
[27]Ibid.

The teacher who was serving as acting principal in the school's seventh year felt that the teachers welcomed his willingness, compared to his predecessor's, to "deal in nitty-gritty." He believed that the staff had been trying to do policy and implementation both collectively, but that they were separable, and that "even if policy, budget, and personnel can be set collectively, there is no reason implementation has to be done that way."[28]

Thus, for a number of reasons—changes in personnel, changes in social environment, and just fatigue on the part of those who had been in from the beginning—the internal governance of the school evolved away from collective decision-making. The teachers were still formally in charge of policy, but they made less of their authority. The passions of the early years, which had led some teachers to leave and some teachers, not necessarily a wholly different group, to think of it as a "peak experience," had abated.

Finally, another event that tended to sever the teaching environment of the Model School from its first beginnings was the physical remodeling of the school building.

The building in which the school had been housed was, as noted, one of the older and more deteriorated in the system. The first group of teachers had arrived at the school before the opening of the term with tools and paints and had made their classrooms distinctively their own. Now, in 1976, the school system moved to remodel the building. The whole old section of the school was gutted and rebuilt, and a new gymnasium and library were added. Classes were regrouped; the original arrangement had all primary grades in one building and all intermediate grades in the other; now classes from grades one to six were grouped in clusters called *family groupings*.

[28]Interview, April 7, 1969.

The teachers had looked forward to the renovation, but somehow, there was a sense of disappointment. Changing the physical environment made a new reality. As one teacher said, "You have to be more careful. . . . It's a showcase."[29] There was not much participation by the teachers in renovation planning. It came at a time when people were beginning to get burnt out and "I didn't know what those drawings meant. Once you get an architect, [there's] not much you could say. Felt sort of bad when they changed the whole character of the second floor."[30] As often happens when a client is an institutional one, those who would use the building found that the design decisions had been made in a way that seemed convenient to the architects but seemed out of fit with their daily practice: a bulletin board set up to be viewed by a whole class, instead of where a small working group of children could use it, sinks located at the convenience of the plumbers. "The kids were so disappointed."

The mixed-grade "family groupings" never really took off and developed a sense of common interest, like that which might tie together teachers of the same grade level or of the same subject matter. The sense of artificiality in this organization added its bit to the various forces that had tended to disperse the sense of collectivity of the early days and to isolate each teacher in her or his own classroom.

In summary, the Model School has, in the years since its founding, become less passionate, less participatory in its governance, and less a community. The principal attributes the more sedate feel of the school to the turnover in teachers: "The staff is different." He cites a study showing that the "starter-uppers" of any institution are a different sort of peo-

[29]Interview, April 7, 1969.
[30]Interview, April 17, 1969.

ple from the "continuers," and he concludes, "We have the continuers."[31]

This may be part of it, but the changes that have taken place both in the way the school is managed and in its external environment—these being, of course, interrelated—seem sufficient to explain much of the difference between the new teachers and the founding group, especially since these changes are paralleled by changes in work life of those who still remain from the early days. As new teachers came in, they entered a school that was no longer controversial in the community but at the same time no longer stood as the expression of a lively movement for "alternative education." As the special relationship to the original consulting group was given up, there were no longer the Gattegno workshops to serve as a means of giving all teachers both a common educational repertoire and a shared experience. As the staff got tired of the endless meetings and began to govern by delegating, there were no longer the endless meetings to link people in shared struggle. No program was developed to instruct new teachers in the special practices of the school, or to transmit the story of the early struggles.

Even in the early days, perhaps especially for the committed teachers of the early days, there was always an underlying conflict between the idea of teacher control as institutional management and the idea of teacher control as the power to run one's classroom in one's own way. Interest in participatory management was lost not just because "the teachers got tired of doing everything"[32] but also because "people were feeling that they were being torn away from

[31]Interview, April 24, 1969.
[32]Interview, April 24, 1969.

teaching by all the meetings."[33] Classroom control won out over institutional management.

Thus, the teacher-controlled Model School has come to be one in which the boundary between each classroom and the rest of the school is more, rather than less, sharp than in the ordinary school. We had an astonishing example during our study: A science teacher, just at the end of the day, had an explosion in an experiment with a fire extinguisher and got badly burned. While he ran out yelling and went to the medical center, the other teachers and their classes stayed in their classrooms; none of them came out to look.[34]

There is a legacy from the early days, however, that serves to increase the responsibility of the individual teacher. There is an idea of being special, a tradition of excellence, that is connected with the practice of teaching from specially developed materials that children are able to work with as individuals or in very small groups. This practice makes for an extraordinary burden of work for any teacher who takes these ideas seriously.

As one teacher explained,

> You have to make up all your material. The teacher will make comments on each paper by each child, which, if each child does two papers a day, makes over fifty papers to comment on. In addition, there must be material for three reading groups and two math groups. Follow-up lessons should be specifically germane to the day before. Almost all of this must be done at home. Teachers have very little free time during the day: teachers in the upper grades are working on special programs even when the specialist has the class at gym.[35]

---

[33]Interview, April 14, 1969.
[34]Interview, June 6, 1969.
[35]Interview, June 6, 1969.

Teacher control thus turns out to be a very curious kind of freedom indeed.

A DAY WITH GEORGIANA

To give something of the taste of the heavy burden that such freedom places on the teacher, here is a day with a highly skilled and particularly committed first-grade teacher at the Model School.

Georgiana has developed to an extraordinary degree the educational practices for which the Barton Model School stands. These make an interesting classroom for children, but a stringent life for the teacher.

Teaching is nowhere easy; it is a kind of people work in which the worker must use himself or herself as an instrument: engaged but not spontaneous. There are both problems of control and intellectual problems of organizing material.

In the usual classroom situation, teachers limit these costs of the work in a number of ways. Control in managed by social forms that establish authority. (The teacher's raised desk at the front of the room dominates the class. Children call the teacher Miss Smith and she calls them John and Mary. Children are taught to remain silent unless called on.) The intellectual problems are partly dealt with by the use of pre-prepared course units, workbooks, and the like. The sense of being always onstage is managed by getting off from time to time—when the children go to gym or art or assembly, or sometimes even during a work period, when it is possible to snatch a quick cigarette and chat in the teachers' room.

Georgiana permits herself none of these devices. Because she feels that her classroom is solely her responsibility, she works extraordinarily hard. Because she uses herself as her working instrument, she is terribly hard on herself. She is at the same time engaged and impersonal, a means to the work of teaching. And because her way of teaching involves presenting children with educational materials that allow them to learn individually or in small groups, she must keep herself at all times alert to what is going on in a very complicated classroom.

In contrast to the traditional classroom, with its clear massing of "pupils" in one area faced by the teacher in the position of authority, Georgiana has her classroom arranged in a series of "centers" where various activities can be carried on. There is a group of tables and little chairs where pupils can do paperwork; there is a "playhouse" corner; there is an area for painting; there is an area with blackboards; and next to the entrance is a shelf with a "minimuseum" of Korean objects, relevant to the main unit of study at the time of my visit. There is no thronelike desk from which the teacher drills and supervises the students; this teacher's rule is more indirect. Her desk is near the entrance corner, but it seems to be used for working rather than surveillance; that she does by looking around from whatever center she is in. If she wants to speak with the children as a group, she calls them to "come to the rug" in the center where the books are. The Big Chair in the room is a rocker, not sacred to the teacher's occupancy; children, alone or in twos, often rock and read in it.

Children usually work alone or in groups of peers. They work in this sense independently, but they do not work spontaneously. What they are to work on and the way in which they are to do it have been programmed by Georgiana, and she watches sharply to see that the materials are used in the educational way for which they were intended.

I arrived at 9:15A.M. Because of the way schools adjust their starting time to the bus schedules, the school day is just beginning. Georgiana is sorting slides; she says she dumped the carousel. Children are coming into the room quietly in ones and twos. They go to take the little chairs down from the tables and gather on the rug. Two children are in the rocking chair. Georgiana, sitting on a shelf, says "See if people can get themselves calm." She waits, very quiet and controlled, while the wrigglers settle down and turn to become part of the group.

"I want to mention two centers," she says. There are ink and brushes in the writing center with which the students are to write their Korean names. Then there are the slides. She demonstrates, very clearly and carefully, the use of the projector. Georgiana announces the three groups with which she will work in reading, and in what order.

Now each child selectes an activity, by taking a tag off the board, and goes to carry out the activity. Georgiana starts working with three children on reading via the Gattegno sound and color sheets. The first reading group is followed by two bigger ones in succession; other children are making paintings of a stuffed seagull, doing brush writing, looking at slides, playing house, and doing worksheets.

There are many ways to teach reading. The Gattegno approach derives from Gattegno's basic idea that acquiring and exercising skill should be its own reward. Children should learn that they can sound out any word, however unfamiliar, and get pleasure from that skill—even if the material read tells no story. Thus, much reading work in Georgiana's class focuses on sounding out individual words, many of which (*schist, azure, obnoxious*) are not ones that children are at all likely to use or even to encounter in daily life. There is one "game" in the lesson. Georgiana points up and down the chart to spell out directions for some activity: the children "follow directions." When this is announced, the children wriggle and one says, "I love to 'follow directions.'"

While she uses the pointer on the chart, Georgiana is

keeping a watch on the children around the room, especially on Paul, who is obviously tense and fidgety. In her one aside to me, she whispers that "Paul has been on the Feingold diet [i.e., to reduce hyperactivity], but he's been off it for a week while he was visiting in Florida."

By 11, the noise level of the room is rising. Paul and a friend are stamping around. Georgiana comes over to speak to Paul in a very low voice. Two boys are standing by the big easel of class-composed stories on sheets and giggling as they make nonsense-word substitutions in the texts. Georgiana comes over and quietly sends them off to another activity.

At 11:10, two older girls come in to try—unsuccessfully—to borrow a ball.

Now, Georgiana goes over to the painting corner, re-aligns the seagull paintings, and mops up. It is 11:15, when she gets out sewing materials and sits down on the rug, joined by two girls whom she is helping to sew Korean flags.

On the other side of the room, two children are prepar-ing to duel with rulers. They see me looking at them and put their rulers against the wall.

Paul is stamping around looking very tense. Georgiana asks him, "Did you do your paper? Did you do a good job on it? Did you put your name on it?"

Now Georgiana, for the first time using a loud, attention-commanding tone, says, "May I have everyone's attention?" She reminds them that "the papers need to be done."

Georgiana is again talking to Paul in a low voice. He goes to play in the "Korean house." Georgiana resumes helping with sewing flags. But she keeps watch on Paul, who is evi-dently having some problems with the other children in the "Korean house." Georgiana sends two girls to tell Paul he must come to see her.

Georgiana says, "John, please come and fix the upside-down slides."

At 11:45, Georgiana gets up and puts away the sewing.

She tells a group of girls to go around cleaning up the room. She herself kneels down by the slide projector and runs through the slides.

At 11:50, she announces it is time to wash hands. The children gather on the rug. Georgiana says, "I'd like to say something about two centers." In the slide center, the children are not to take the slides out. In the "Korean house," "You are supposed to do things you have learned can be done there. Some things aren't acceptable there." She also announces that there is a flag to be claimed that evidently fell from the white table.

Georgiana now reads a Korean fairy story. For the first time, she seems a bit unsure; she asks the children whether she read it before. Or perhaps Mrs. Kim told it when she came.

Now comes lineup and the designation of which children are to do which tasks at lunch. All go down the hall to the lunchroom. Georgiana eats with the children, then follows them out of doors for a short recess in the drizzle.

At 1:00, the children and Georgiana are back in the room. "It's quiet time," Georgiana says to me. Some children are sitting at tables, mostly reading. Some have their heads down. Georgiana moves about quietly, sitting with one and another, listening to their reading. Children go to and fro, quietly getting and returning books. A girl of ten or twelve comes in quietly and borrows a game. A mother arrives with a box.

At 1:30 Georgiana announces, "I want everyone to put his or her things away and come over to the rug." It is Kristin's last day. There is a present, which another child carries to Kristin. It seems to be pictures of the children in the class. Refreshments are served—Hi-C and doughnuts. The children consume these at their tables—the party seems rather dispersed.

Back at the rug at 1:45, Georgiana reminds the children

that last Thursday Mrs. Kim came and brought cookies. She asks for volunteers to write letters to Mrs. Kim thanking her. As it works out, about everyone seems to be writing such letters. Georgiana displays the conventional form of indentation and spells some words on the board.

At 2:00, Karen, the counselor, comes in and one girl goes off with her. Georgiana mentions Paul's tension to the counselor.

By 2:20, things are getting a little noisy again, especially because the girls in the "Korean house" are playing rather noisily.

At 2:30 comes music time. The children line up and go down the hall to the music room, where the music teacher, standing at an upright, whangs out the accompaniment to some Korean songs, which—it is announced—the children will sing at the coming open house. Georgiana is actively involved in this lesson, too; she moves the children around to sing.

There is a difference from the classroom, though. In her interactions with the music teacher is the first time I have seen Georgiana really break into a smile.

Back at the room, everyone gathers on the rug. Georgiana goes over the job list. The children start to put the chairs up. Good-bye is said to Kristin; several children hug her. Georgiana reviews those children who have not finished their flags; who "got to paint." From time to time, the PA gratingly announces a bus ready, and few children go out.

Georgiana puts up the flags.

When I ask Georgiana how long she has been teaching, she says that would be to tell her age. She has been eight years at the Model School. Twenty years altogether, she admits. She started in Montgomery County.

She lives alone. She indicates that a teaching job makes heavy demands on private life.

She values the freedom of the Model School: "Like being

able to do a unit on Korea instead of the usual first-grade unit on Japan."

What rewards keep her going? Both the children's response and learning in the course of preparing the material. She enjoyed finding the material on Korea. In the reading, she knows that so well now it is only the children's response.

Georgiana is a teacher of not only more-than-average skill, but of considerably more-than-average seriousness. Having an observer in the classroom may well have brought both these attributes more sharply than usual into play. Nevertheless, just because Georgiana is at one extreme in the spectrum of Model School teachers, her way of working brings into sharp relief the consequences of worker control when the dominant meaning of control is responsibility for the work.

Georgiana has so thoroughly made her work her own that she does not leave it behind when she leaves the classroom; she goes home to prepare materials for the next day. For Georgiana, control has meant a framing of work in which it has become, both in time and in psychic engagement, most of her life.

The very seriousness and engagement of Georgiana's approach to her work are what makes it satisfying to her. Like the solitary potter who one day tried to see how many mugs she could make and saw that the mugs of that overextended day were the best of all, Georgiana gets a kind of pure, lonely pleasure from her own skill and self-discipline in exercising that skill.

Chapter 5

PRINCIPAL WORK

WITH JOAN WOFFORD

Many white-collar workers would see a school principal's work as very appealing. Principals appear to have ultimate control, autonomy and authority in their own organizations.

Principals can also experience the sense of ownership and belonging usually reserved in the private sector for executives with six-figure incomes. Principals are the ceremonial heads of their organizations; the potential for their emotional involvement with their schools seems limitless.

Of course, the job is not without problems: "It's lonesome at the top." Principals have no real peers or colleagues, only subordinates (teachers, staff) and clients (students, parents). Then, too, principals aren't exactly at the "top." They are usually responsible to administrators in the school system's central office—to rules made "downtown"—to influential parent groups, to influential teacher groups; they are circumscribed by the teachers' contract and must cope with day-to-day problems from vandalism to wounded feelings.

With its odd mix of flexibility and constraint, the work of school principals takes shape as an extreme kind of "people work." The principal we discuss provides insights into an extraordinary commitment to work, which is rewarding to him but hard to define. For him, flexibility and success are vitally important, and the invisibility of successful people-work is a continuing dilemma.

A TYPICAL DAY

What does the principal of a large (seventeen hundred-pupil) and visible suburban high school do? Basically, he works with people to resolve day-to-day problems (with students, teachers, parents, and the central administration); organizes the smooth running of the institution (scheduling, personnel, and budget); supervises teachers (meets with departments and individuals, observes classes); represents the institution in public arenas (PTA meetings, school board meetings, athletic events); and plans long term for its future. He performs these tasks either face-to-face with individuals or groups, on the telephone, or occasionally in writing.

When asked to walk through a typical day, selected, in part, on the basis of a file of five years of weekly lists of things to do, the principal in this study chose a Monday in March 1980. Since what he does on Monday is based, in part, on what he does on Sunday, it is first important to indicate that on this Sunday, as every other Sunday, he said that he

1. Created his week's list of things to do (normally consisting of twelve or so major issues to worry about, a half dozen budget items, about thirty people to see or phone on smaller issues, and a half dozen reports or memos that need to be written.)
2. In addition, he made separate lists for each of the people who report to him (his two assistant princi-

pals, his department chairmen, and his director of buildings and grounds) and a separate list of issues to be taken up with the superintendent.
3. Dictated or wrote memos and letters.
4. Wrote a list to his secretary of the people he wanted to see during that week, for how long, and on what subjects.
5. Prepared for special panels or large meetings.

At 7:30 on Monday morning, he arrived at his office, unpacked his briefcase and filed papers within arm's reach, caught the director of guidance, who usually arrives early, and gave his secretary dictation and a phone list.

8:15–8:45   Met with the chairman of the foreign language department.
8:45–9:00   Met with the clerk to give her directions on how to do a special study of ninth-graders' free periods and where they occurred.
9:00–11:30   Left school to participate in a panel on supervising and evaluating teachers together with the superintendent and the school board president before the Village Club at the town library.
11:30–12:00 Met in a standing appointment with his guidance director to review work on the assignment of all ninth-graders to deans that would happen later in the week and for which task the principal and the guidance director had worked five hours on the previous Saturday.
12:00–12:30 Walked down to the school cafeteria to talk with students.
12:30–1:00   and
1:45–2:00   Telephone calls:

- Called the police chief regarding rumors about drug use at the high school.
- Called the assistant superintendent regarding the dusty walls in the auditorium renovation.
- Called a counselor to follow up on the issue of moving

a youngster into a special class, about which a teacher was complaining.
- Called the PTA president regarding the executive meeting scheduled for that night.
- Called the architect about the renovation because of a problem involving a student and a student's mother, who were claiming that the architect had promised to use a student as a worker on the renovation.

1:00–1:45	Met with a teacher who was in conflict with her department chairman about teaching part time, as the teacher had recently had a baby and wanted to combine teaching and family commitments.
2:00–2:45	Met with teacher to break the news that she was not going to be rehired.
2:45–3:15	Pulled together the plans for a faculty meeting.
3:15–4:15	Faculty meeting.
4:30–5:15	Met with the director of the Alternative school (another school in the system) about trying to involve other teachers in a school democracy grant.
5:15–5:30	Parent phone calls (good time to call parents):

- Called a parent who was complaining about a teacher's treatment of his child (tried to set up student–teacher conference, then teacher–parent conference).
- Called a parent who wanted to make a particular request for his child's dean assignment and had missed the deadline for doing so in writing.

5:30–6:15	Paper work:

- Opened mail and distributed it.
- Signed letters and forms.
- Sorted phone call slips.
- Returned more phone calls.

6:15–8:00	Got home, ran, ate supper.
8:00	PTA executive council meeting.

What product does this principal have to show for his fifteen-hour day? What evidence does he have—and what evidence does he feel that others have—that he has worked, and worked effectively?

The high school principal under consideration has met regularly over five years with a consultant for the purpose of learning by examining his own practice—looking closely at what he does and how he thinks and feels about what he does. The interactions that provide him both a support system and a focus for his personal growth have been audiotaped and transcribed. The words of the principal quoted in this paper are drawn from the transcriptions of those five years of tapes.

In the early years of his principalship, Dan engaged in a helter-skelter, ad hoc pattern of responding to the range of demands. Of that period, he said:

> I just kept going at a frenzied pace. I realized that I wasn't being effective. . . . I've got to find ways to do fine this situation. . . .

> I go jogging. It's hard for me to let myself walk; I feel as if I disappoint myself when I do. . . . I try to run at a pace that really pushes me. . . . I don't pay attention to little things that bother me—my foot hurts or something like that. I ignore that. . . .

> It's really elusive. . . . What do I work for? Partly, it's really wanting to make things better for the kids. . . . I really want to succeed; I don't want to survive. I mean I do want to survive, but it's not that kind of a feeling. I've set up these standards for success for myself, the job, that I really commit myself to. . . . In the last job I had, I got enough success so that I was able to keep it going. But I'm not getting that here, I'm not getting the feeling of whatever affirms those goals. . . . I have a lot of the little things I cherish, but none of the big things. The little things are limited change, educational reform—

those kinds of things. . . the need for power, the desire
to control, money . . . what I picture is myself picking
up these things in my hands, and their being small, not
being things which . . . Is that the kind of thing that I
want in my life? How I want to spend my time and my
energy? What makes me feel good, makes me feel as if
it's worth it? I feel that tension.

This is a job where you can do anything you want.
And you won't exhaust it; it'll exhaust you. More demands on your emotional energy, your time. I took the
principalship of the middle school . . . as far as it would
go. I extended it to its limit. Of course, in the process, I
got tired.

See, it's hard for me to say no. I just haven't learned
how to do it. One of the reasons I never go to lunch is
that I feel guilty about it. I feel as if I ought to be in
school, and I can find ways to spend the time working,
that's for sure.

At this point, the public pressures on the principal and
the responsive internal pressures within Dan kept him from
finding a satisfying balance between his own need for flexibility and his need to be obviously and actively accountable. As
time went on, Dan became more able to slow down and get a
perspective on the pressures of the job without jumping in to
respond to them.

Being a Slave of My List of Things to Do
And I'm going to be spending July doing the scheduling. . . . There's a tremendous pressure for day-to-day
sort of tasks that have to be done, that I think is incredi-
ble. I understand why the last two principals of this high
school became alcoholics. I mean, the job literally destroyed those two guys. From that perspective, the only
reason it hasn't done that to me is that I'm more re-
sourceful than they were. (*Pause.*) It's a combination of
tasks that any principal in a high school has to be ultimately responsible for and the high pressure of the community—in terms of the demand for quality and the
demand for service for particular problems. I probably

spend two hours a day on parent problems, and I deal
with them well; that's why it's two hours. If I didn't, it
might be even *more*. That would also create a whole
other set of pressures. You know what I mean? I mean,
from my perspective, I do a hell of a job. And I don't
know how much longer I want to do it, in that hard,
driving, sort of one-problem-after-another kind of way,
acting on incomplete information all the time. . . .
(*Laughs.*) Being a slave of my list of things to do.

Some interesting themes emerge here. If the job of handling a distraught parent is done well, the parent may never
fully realize how well handled she or he was, others may not
realize what the principal did, and the principal will end up
simply having more time to handle more emergencies. The
higher quality of the "people work," then, the more likely it
is to disappear. If the parent feels "handled," she or he may
feel manipulated, and that either creates mistrust or ends up
taking more time. Instead, the parent has to feel genuinely
heard and responded to. If she or he goes away satisfied, the
principal then has more time to respond to more parents. If
the parent is not satisfied, the problem swells to take up still
more time and to create new problems.

One criterion, then, of effective "people work" is the
quantity of people problems solved that stay solved. Therefore, one measure of effectiveness is volume. Perhaps for this
reason, the principal immediately points to his calendar,
which is fuller than his boss's:

How I Know I'm Busy
You know, I look at the superintendent and I say,
"He's not under the same tension as I am day to day. He
has a longer term sort of problems, maybe a week or a
few days, but he *rarely* has to formulate immediate
things under that kind of pressure." And you know how
I know that? I know that from his calendar. My calendar
is much fuller than his. When he's unavailable, it's because he's at a meeting somewhere; otherwise, you can

usually find him in his office and get some time with him. That's not to say he's not busy and doesn't work hard; he has all these nights and weekends.

Yet, in another part of himself, the principal is suspicious of himself when he is busy. He does not trust the business nor does he fully trust the forces in him that resist it, which he fears as signs of burnout or cynicism:

Fear of Burnout
 I feel less energetic, I feel less willing to extend myself now than I did in the job a while ago. There's a part of me that feels good about that. There's another part of me that scares me, because I feel that whole burned-out sort of thing. I have given so much energy to my job over the last ten years. How much longer can I do that?

Fear of Cynicism
 And, you know, as you become more aware of the limits on what can happen in an organization in any sort of lasting way, and as you become more realistic in that way, there's a cynicism that also develops—for me, at least—that *scares* me.

Another force pushing him to be less busy is the side of himself that is reflective and yearns for contemplation. This side he trusts:

The Need for Reflection
 I have a friend whom I met in sixth grade. And we had a "separate peace"; we had a Gene–Phineas relationship in high school. I think I was the Gene to his Phineas. . . . We both went to Harvard and we roomed together freshman year. Then, we sort of grew apart after that. I hadn't seen him for a while, but I saw him over Christmastime. During some part of the conversation. . . he said, "Who else but your school would hire a scholarly administrator?" And I was really pleased with that. And I felt good that he would describe me that way. And there's part of me that would like to have

more of that kind of life, you know, a balance to the active, problem-solving nature of these jobs . . . more contemplation. One of the things I like about these times of meeting with you [the consultant], these spaces, is that I can take a particular issue and really look at it in all of its dimensions, and I get a feel for it that I don't ever get any other way in the daily turmoil. I would like to do that with everything I have. . . . So I have that sort of yearning. And I get very impatient with a lot of the stuff that I might have found interesting at one point; it's just boring to me now. It just has to get done, paperwork stuff. So . . . (*Sighs.*)

Around November I sat down and started to write some stuff. I really felt good about it; I got excited about it. And then I lost the time. I did it right after Thanksgiving. I wrote about fifteen pages and got it typed. . . . I felt really good about it, that I'd done it, but then I dropped it. I would have liked to be able to continue that.

I wish I had more time to talk with other people who've faced the same kind of issues in their personal and professional lives. . . . I value this; I wish I had more time for this. I wish I had more time to formulate things that I think the faculty may be ready for—part of this sense of potential power is the feeling that if I have the time to do it well, I could make some changes in the high school. So I wish I had. And part of that has to do with that fifteen-page thing I wrote. . . . And I don't have the time to do it. I don't find the time to do it, within the limits I put on the job.

Here, we see Dan responding to the dilemma of valuing his role for its potential creativity, yet getting bogged down in the monotony of daily tasks. He valued the chance to talk and share but had not yet found how to define his job in such a way as to permit him to be reflective, other than with a consultant.

If one way to judge effectiveness in people work is in terms of quantity and speed, how did the principal reconcile his sense that reflection and contemplation might produce more lasting contributions if only he could define his job in such a way as to carve out that time? One response he gave was to supervise and delegate effectively:

The Best Side of Me: Delegation
> . . . I feel pride in these people (my subordinates) being able to do their thing well. I have a sense of having shared a lot of stuff in my job.
>
> I feel as if I've taken this best side of me and applied it to a really chaotic, disorganized mess and made a coherence out of it for the school, for teachers, and for the program. I've made a whole series of decisions, hiring decisions, other decisions. . . . And the smooth running of the school this year is a reflection of this.
>
> . . . And I'm clear about the things I want to keep to myself, like parents, relations to the PTA, curriculum planning, program issues, (a teaching load, contact with teachers, even with kids.) I did a thing with the board, and at the end of it, one of the principals said, "You ought to be a teacher."

The Worst Side of Me: Feeling I've Given My Job Away
> So that's me at my best. And then my worst is feeling insecure, [feeling] a sense of "I've given my job away." You know, people don't tend to see me anymore; they go to the vice-principal or the chairmen. They don't have a feeling of legitimacy because I'm not dealing with those day-to-day things in the way I was. Someone mentioned to me yesterday that feeling of the first day, the day before school opened, when nobody came to him and said, "This has got to be done; I *need you* so that school can open!" That feeling of not being essential is a *powerful* thing to deal with. . . .
>
> And I know I could put this all on the positive side, too. But I'm feeling it negatively. I bet that as I get older, I'll get more aware of my needs . . . to control. I guess in some ways I can intellectualize it as coming from my insecurity, that I'm feeling that, because I see them as connected. You know, I'm feeling good about myself.

But on the other side of that, I feel that I'm losing control—if you can make this distinction.

It gets hard to sort out sometimes, too. It's hard to know when I *should* be asserting more control. Where are the legitimate places for me, as I'm redefining this job, to express my principalship?

I feel the competitiveness with my vice-principal on the negative side powerfully. One of the places it gets to be a problem with me is around, for instance—Did I tell you the details of my blowup with the superintendent about personal leave? Yeah, I did. Well, I came back from that meeting feeling like "Son of a bitch, I've really got to watch those personal leave applications, because this is going to be my procedure, and I don't want to get caught, for a whole variety of reasons." So I went back to the vice-principal and said to him, "I'm going to have to take over those things." And he's been doing them. He's the reward system. I made the allocations in travel money to the departments. . . . My instinct was that I should be doing that, but I had given that over and I needed to take it back. I wouldn't have done that if this hadn't happened with the superintendent about one teacher.

But there was another part of me that was sort of saying, "Oh shit, at least I'll get this part of my job back." (*Laughs.*)

Here the same dilemma inherent in people work is apparent. To delegate and supervise effectively is, again, to become invisible. In order to escape this dilemma in part, the principal found it necessary to retain parts of his job and to become more visible in certain areas.

Thus far, we have seen that Dan responded to the dilemma involving the limitations on work by learning to plan his priorities and activities (his lists) and by delegating responsibility (his subordinates). These structures were not totally satisfying as reflected in his resentment of the lists ("being a slave") and his fears about delegation ("feeling I've given my job away"). However, these structures do appear to have enabled him to enjoy his job and not be destroyed by it, as were his predecessors.

Yet the burden of shaping his week (and taking part of every Sunday to do so) takes its toll. It is not easy to learn to say no (which it is time he does) and to make that "no" publicly acceptable to the diverse constituencies who watch him or to the jogger within him who used to find it hard to walk. The burden of shaping his work week expresses itself in fatigue, or worry about burnout.

If to be effective in people work is to be trapped in the paradox of invisibility, what happens when a good "people worker" is deliberately visible? One of the outcomes is to behave in such a way as to cause puzzlement, at best, and dislike, at worst.

Slowing Them Down When They Want Action Leads to Puzzlement
I've had some other tremendous success this year. My last faculty meeting, in fact. (*Pause.*) Well, it's a long story. (*Laughs.*) I'm not going to tell the whole story. But briefly, it's about a policy we've taken. I made a proposal about changing that policy . . . there was a lot of emotion around it. Arguments were presented for and against it. They just seemed to go right into it; they were really tough about it. I tried to focus on the issue and keep it narrow enough so it was possible to debate.

In fact, they got a little ahead of me. I came in not planning to vote on it, and somebody proposed that we vote. Then, I had to make some decisions quickly about how to let that happen. In fact, there was some confusion about it that I thought I could clear up. I was hesitant because it wasn't written down—this change I had made—and I thought it was important that it *be* written down.

So, one teacher said, "Let's get a sense of how people feel about this." So what I said was "Let's first do this; then let's do that. There seems to be some feeling, but let's be clear about what the vote means. Let's assume the vote is strongly positive. . . . This won't be enacted as a decision until the following things have happened. I'll put this in writing and put it in your mailboxes. Then, we'll have two kinds of meetings between now and the time it will be enacted. One with the faculty representatives of departments in a group that meets with me, and then, we'll have another faculty meeting. At that point, I'll ask of people have considered this and want to open the question before we go ahead and put it in our red book."

That puzzled people. They said afterward, "Why did you do that?" I think what they thought was that here I was carrying the day (by proposing something) and then I was backing away from it.

Here, the principal carefully placed structures around an action that the faculty was eager to take. Presumably, the structures were his way of making operational a commitment to the importance of framing the discussion within a process of decision making and giving a rationale in terms of the difficulty of achieving clarity and the importance of not rushing decisions. Yet, the result for others was puzzlement. When they were eager to act, he juxtaposed the values of reflection, clarity, and procedures. They did not know how to make sense of that; yet he felt wonderful about himself and termed it a "tremendous success."

I Have a Lot More Power Than I Had Before

I didn't expect it to go so well. And the other quality that impressed me was that the teachers were not suspicious . . . I mean, there was immediate support. There was less nonsense about me going on. I was less an issue and I felt a sense—as I do in a variety of ways— of being accepted. (*Pause.*) That's been consistent; I've talked about that before. But it pleases me that I'm not an issue—my motives, my strategies. . . .

I feel as if I have a lot more—in a positive way— power than I had before. I think if I stayed there a while longer, I might be able to—because of the way I've pre-

sented myself to the faculty—do some things that I really want to do, that I've wanted to do; it's just taken time,
three and a half years. . . . Even if I had the skills to do
that [what he did in the group meeting] a few years ago,
it wouldn't have worked the same way. The group let
me turn it around.

His skills, his acceptance by the faculty, and his increased
power—all make it more possible for him to do what he did in
the faculty meeting, yet even while feeling accepted by the
faculty, he encountered puzzlement and dislike and, with
them, also loneliness. What he said was:

It's the Loneliest Job in the World
One of the ways this job does not interact with my
needs is that I'm not well liked. I want to be loved and
approved of. But I put limits on things, and at best,
people are ambivalent about that. One respected teacher
told me, "You've made it with the faculty; they're back
to arguing policy."

It's the loneliest job in the world. I have no colleagues; I'm the only person in the system who reports
directly to the superintendent; the elementary principals
have each other. I tried to develop a collegial relationship with my assistant principal, but it didn't work.

I discovered two important limits of the principalship as I experienced it. The first was that no matter how
much I yearned for collegueship, I was essentially
alone. When I was teaching some years ago in a large
suburban school, I remember a teacher I respected saying that the principal must be one of the loneliest people
in the world. I've had that offhand, chance remark from
long ago confirmed so often in my work.

If when he does the job well he is invisible and when he
is visible he is unliked, what keeps a person like this principal
working at his job? What safisfactions and pleasures does he
get?

One of his answers suggests that he cares passionately

about the idea of the high school as an institution and about the values for which it has stood:

My Role: Speaking for the Values of the Institution

I see my role as being one who speaks for the values of the institution, who communicates that those are things people can have, hope for, aspire to, have faith in. In the past, people accepted high schools and believed in them. That faith has been shaken, moved from impersonal transactions to personal ones; moved from institutional authority to personal authority. Teachers were hired for their personal credibility with kids and because they could meet individual needs. Personal authority won't hold the institution together; we need a new kind of institutional authority, which I am defining and putting forth, an integration of personal and institutional authority.

That's my job: to reclaim a place for the institution as legitimate for teachers, students, and parents. But not the old institution, which was too standardized and uniform and didn't recognize the people's needs. The new one has to stand for something and apply precedents and consistency and have policies that force people to give up individual rights and freedom and needs in the interest of community rights and freedom and needs. I see my commitment in organizational terms.

I want to create a public arena that is committed to the fair resolution of conflict; to decentralize the power away from me and put it out where it can be seen as a credible part of the institution so the institution can be seen as fair and provide outlets for conflict resolution. That's a redefinition of the institution. I am working to find new structures by which to return to the institution its legitimate authority.

One of the nicest things that's come out of my job is a clearer sense of what I should be working on. I am no longer casting around for what to be working on, in fits and starts. I now have hold of something that gives it meaning, not just high-level maintenance.

When I say no to someone, I can fit it into a structure. There's a reason to say no, and it relates to the last problem I said no to, and that coherence has meaning for me.

I see the seamy side, the cynicism of the staff. I get discouraged. Having a central idea gives me a lift, a balance.

I have less of a sense of my job as a lot of little fragments and more of a sense of my representing some sort of stabilizing force in the school that stands for something and acts on a certain set of values; more of a sense of how difficult that is and more of a sense of my own inadequacy.

But I feel a sense of strength in a central idea.

A final dilemma noted for people who make their own work has to do with work as an expression of personal values or politics. Here, we see Dan finding central meaning in his work through his growing capacity to speak for what he sees to be the central values of the institution. This sense of a larger context for himself contrasts sharply with his earlier sense of power, control, and money as the little things that in themselves did not constitute satisfying work.

In a more humorous, less philosophical vein, he described a faculty meeting:

The Fun Side

Let me give you an example of the whole faculty, at the same meeting. The first item on my agenda was Christmas parties. . . . I used to be so terrorized by standing up in front of that group that I would literally write down everything I was going to say. It would take me hours; I would write a speech, or a set of speeches, word for word. I didn't trust myself to improvise at all. So I would spend Sundays before faculty meetings, or a big *part* of Sunday, writing out everything I wanted to say. Some of the criticism I heard about it that hurt me deeply at one point was that people would say (I got most of this indirectly), "We don't want to be preached to or lectured to. We want to be involved in meetings."

And I felt that in my preparation I had ways to involve people, but that it just didn't come up.

The other feedback I got was that I was stiff and uncomfortable, which was true. (*Laughs.*) Well, I feel more relaxed this year. So I hadn't really planned what to say about these Christmas parties, except a teacher had said to me, "Can't we just hold them until the last day or two before Christmas, instead of all these parties all week and kids going nuts, and noise, and mess?" So I started to talk about it; I just started to have some fun with it. I said I realized how much these parties mean to the teachers, and how important it is for kids to have seven or eight Christmas parties in a row over three or four days in the last week of school. (*Laughs.*) And people started to chuckle and laugh about it. And I just got playing that out, that sarcasm.

Well, the teachers laughed and no one said anything. Then someone said, "In the language department, we teach other cultures, and we need to bring in food of other nationalities. This is part of the curriculum." And the whole place just went, "Ohhhh." Then, another guy said, "I was planning to cook a Christmas goose for my class." And I said, "Friday for the Christmas goose." (*Laughs.*) And then this kooky woman said, "Well, my freshman seminar group has been planning a party for the Tuesday before Christmas vacation since September. Can we go ahead with it?" And she ended up by saying, "And your daughter's in that group." Then the place roared, and I said, "You handle the other kids and I'll handle my daughter." (*Laughs.*)

Well, I tell you some of that because—the chairman of the English Department, the most esteemed member of our staff in some ways, said the next day that he was very pleased that I was so relaxed in the faculty meetings, and that I'd really changed. So, I feel a lot better about that.

The two things I feel best about are (1) a procedural thing that works, that suggests to teachers a kind of civic responsibility for how a large group can work, and (2) when I reach them emotionally, when there isn't a dry

eye in the place, I loved that. I love to reach them emotionally because I don't see it very often.

What appears to give this principal the greatest pleasure
are further examples of his growing competence as an effective people-worker: his capacity to structure interactions in
such a way as to embody a set of values important to him,
and the ability out of his own personal skills to teach people
emotionally.

CONCLUSION

Over the course of five years of regular and recorded
reflection on his evolving leadership style, Dan, the principal
of a large suburban high school, has experienced a number of
the dilemmas of successful people work. Initially, he struggled with creating the internal boundaries that enabled him
to limit his job for himself and "to learn to walk," not always
run. As he succeeded, he developed the confidence to place
external limits on his job by delegating more of his tasks to
subordinates and freeing himself for more reflective work.
Yet, as he delegated successfully, he confronted the fears of
being administratively invisible. While his reflective and conceptual contributions provided new ways to limit his job—to
say no—time for reflection was threatened by the old, pressing demands of the job. His conceptual leadership—combined with increasing skills in group management—enabled
him to structure faculty decision-making; yet, in setting limits
on the faculty, he engendered their resistance and ambivalence.

This, then, has been the story of an individual's increasing competence in people work and of the tensions that ac-
company the success that he has attained.

Chapter 6

THE NEW ENGLAND FOOD CO-OP

Mixed Motives in Collective Work

WITH RUSS TANNER

The New England Food Co-op (NEFCO) is a warehouse owned and run by more than a hundred consumer-food cooperatives in New Hampshire, eastern Massachusetts, and southern Maine. The warehouse buys grains, cheeses, produce, and other products by the truckload; stores them; and resells them to member co-ops at a small markup.

The food co-ops are both practical and political—and, in each aspect, part of an American historical tradition. They must get food to their members more cheaply than the supermarket, and while there is a certain political implication to beating the companies at their own game, in this practical

127

bottom line the co-ops draw on a long and thoroughly bourgeois cooperative tradition. But the food co-ops also came into being as part of the radical movements of the 1960s, with their search for democratic and participatory social alternatives: the movement "Red Rudi" Dutschke called "the long march through the institutions."

The warehouse is a cooperative, since it is owned by its member co-ops, but it is run by a staff that the board of directors hires as a collective; that is, the staff is responsible to the board as a whole, rather than as individual employees. There is no manager, and each staff member is formally on an equal footing with the others. It is this nonhierarchical, collective nature of the warehouse staff that makes the work environment at NEFCO interesting: a small organization (the full-time staff have always been less than twelve) where the workers make many of the decisions that shape their own work—what it is and how it gets done.

The staff have control over daily functions, such as purchasing, cash flow, and work hours, and they set their own salary, while the board, with strong input from the staff, makes major policy decisions, such as the fees charged to co-ops or major purchases. Buying a small van is within the authority of the staff, while going into the trucking business is not.

Because it is collective, working at NEFCO is a kind of political statement. It succeeds to the degree that work is done and operational decisions are made by a group lacking formal authority and hierarchy, and having a minimum of role specialization. In the way that NEFCO workers move between paperwork and heavy physical labor, there is something of an echo—an echo carried by the political currents of the 1960s—of Marx's dream of work as a chosen activity.

But NEFCO is also a multi-million-dollar business with a lot of physical labor, paperwork, and cash flow, as well as constant decision-making. The collective organization must carry this work load, and do so well enough to realize the practical bottom line represented by the economic competition of the large food distributors.

Small businesses with alternative forms of management and ownership are forming all the time; however, NEFCO is particularly worth studying because the business is more than five years old, has been growing rapidly, and has even been turning a small profit. An auditor attributed this profit largely to the high productivity of the small, committed staff. Staff members—wholly responsible for running the warehouse—have taken on motivation and commitment to the business expected only of managers, while performing both management tasks and routine physical/clerical jobs. The collective staff seem to be quite successful at performing both kinds of jobs at once, although not without some difficulties. They have faced many problems and decisions associated with rapid growth and changing function and still remain a financially stable organization.

"Why would someone want to go crazy working in a collective warehouse for three years?" one staff member rhetorically asked during an interview. The answer is certainly not material rewards, since the hours are long and pay ends up being around minimum wage. There are no opportunities for advancement. The work itself is frequently routine and monotonous, and sometimes unpleasant. Yet they are highly motivated workers.

PERSONAL POLITICS

As the profiles below help illustrate, much of the staff's motivation is based on personal politics and a feeling that the job is furthering social change. Most of the staff come from the ranks of member food co-ops and have a deep commitment to them. They see their job at NEFCO as helping the food co-ops to continue and grow. Perhaps as important a

motivation to NEFCO workers is the experiment of working
in a collectively run business. Again, this is partly a political
motivation; a belief in the value of a nonhierarchical workplace and a desire to experience that belief. Certainly, the
actual control of one's workplace is a strong work incentive.
Comments like "The boss on my last job was an asshole" and
"I had to find a job where I was more in control" were common in interviews, but also, just running the warehouse as a
collective, with no managers, is a goal in itself, aside from the
improvement in individual working lives. Whatever the degree of success they achieve, they have at least given a democratic workplace a good try.

One staff member said,

> Co-ops come out of a community direction, breaking
> down the structures that are there . . . on the other
> hand, I don't give a shit about food. My focus from the
> beginning was "What does it mean to be a collective?"
> that's one of the things I'm really interested in around
> here.

Another said,

> There were a lot of personal philosophy issues. I
> couldn't work in something that I disagreed with politi-
> cally, and my job had to be more pragmatic, had to deal
> with people's need to survive.
>   My whole idealistic notion is that work is life . . . at
> least, that's the way I want my life to be.

Many NEFCO workers have had previous job careers
and college educations that probably would not have led
them to work in a warehouse if not for their interest in its
politics. Yet, while politics is a big part of NEFCO's environment, on a daily, functional basis it is not necessarily a main
motivation for warehouse workers.

The following comments by the staff member who had
been there the longest begin to illustrate this point:

> I was attracted by the decision-making process here. I
> thought the collective was real interesting. Now, I'm not
> sure that I'm the kind of person who's good in this situa-
> tion. . . . I think a lot of us came into the job with certain
> ideas that motivated us, but they fade and you find
> other things to keep you going.

Just what those "other things" are is very complicated
and different for each person. The personal environment,
competency and skill, and a commitment to keeping the business running seem to be the strongest and most common.

PERSONAL MOTIVATION

It seems to have been characteristic of almost all of the
staff to develop strong personal relationships—frequently extending beyond warehouse time—and motivation from these
relationships. As one relatively new staff member put it,
"You are difficult to replace in the collective, and there's a lot
of pressure not to let other people down . . . it's kind of like
the love motivation." This is also reflected in the biannual
staff retreats, which, in part, are a time for staff members to
"just relax with each other."

All of the workers at NEFCO talk about the importance
of the personal environment to their motivation and as a
support mechanism. There is a lot of friendship among the
staff, and it is always more enjoyable to work with your
friends. This is reflected in the emphasis on working in informal teams, as well as in the almost constant conversations
among the people working, frequently about NEFCO matters. The personal environment also creates a sense of shared
plight, and this is very supportive:

> The friendship aspect is very important now. It
> wasn't why I started it, but it helps keep me going. . . . I
> tell myself a lot I want to make it better for the other
> people who work here.

> The work is hard to keep up with—it's like being a housewife, no matter how many times you clean the floor, it gets dirty. That's probably the most negative part of the job, but then you're not isolated in that, and that's positive.

Much of the work is hard physical labor, which, done alone, could be experienced as extremely burdensome. However, at NEFCO, there is a definite attempt to share such tasks in a way that makes them a convivial and socially bonding experience.

For example, Sharon, the writer, and a co-op volunteer were working in the warehouse trying to maneuver an oil drum into position on a pouring rack so that the cooking oil could be poured into smaller containers. It took all three of us to get it into position and opened; then, the volunteer began the tedious job of pouring. Sharon said regretfully to him, "I guess it's just going to be you pouring the oil. I've got to be somewhere else. I'll come by from time to time to see how you're doing."

Other jobs don't turn out to be so solitary, even when they might easily be. Cutting cheese, for example, becomes an occasion for helping another worker to press the heavy blade, to weigh the pieces, and to share the crumbs. There is a definite emphasis on working together on most tasks. Sharon's regret at having to leave a worker alone with a tedious job was genuine, and there are many similar examples. People seem to form into informal work teams to do each job, and there are often enough activities going on so that one has a choice as to which team to join.

The warehouse uses no motorized machinery. Instead, the workers use hand-operated pallet jacks to move the pallets, some weighing a thousand pounds or more, from the truck to the elevator and then from the elevator to the proper storage place. Again, workers usually do this job together in order to preserve back muscles and make the task more enjoyable by talking while they push, pull, or lift. The use of muscle power instead of motorized pallet jacks has a certain economic logic at NEFCO (with its low wages), but it also represents an implicit value given to the social bond created by shared manual labor.

COMPETENCY AND SKILL

The informal structure of the co-op, with its absence of formal job ladders, is extraordinarily open to anyone who wants to take on the responsiblility for a particular area requiring specialized skill.

Take the case of Sharon:

Harry (a new staff member): What did you do before you worked here?
Sharon: Oh, raised kids and lived on welfare.

Sharon is the mother of two children, the youngest of whom is now sixteen. It is perhaps because of them that she did antiwar work during the Vietnam war. She joined the Mission Hill food co-op to make it easier to feed them: "For a long time it was enough for me just to be in the co-op. I joined for cheap food (which I think is a valid reason), and then I got really interested in NEFCO." She became involved in NEFCO board meetings and was "enchanted by the consensus system." For a long time, she did the volunteer coordinating, which involves scheduling volunteer workers from co-ops to fit into the peak work loads of the warehouse. She did this herself as a volunteer until she was hired as a full-time worker in June 1977.

Before working with NEFCO, Sharon's only recent paying job had been as a farm laborer the previous summer, picking crops in the field. It was her first paid job in eighteen years. She had been raising her children in the interim. Before that came ten years of jobs: clerk, hospital worker, and typist. "None of them were in management. I never made contracts for thousands of dollars," she notes. "I originally worked here as a volunteer, with little responsibility. A few days after I was hired full time, my emotional state completely changed. I was responsible for the reputation of the co-op. I've lived in a state of emergency ever since."

Sharon is fifty-four, nearly twenty years older than any other worker at the warehouse; yet her age stands out no more than the soft silver streaks in her brown hair. She is as energetic as nearly anyone there. She seems to be neither condescending toward others, nor singled out by others because of her age. There is, however, at least one difference of perspective that she brings into the warehouse because of her age. As she once said when talking about her attraction to collectives, "I'm too old to be told what to do."

Sharon had been involved in NEFCO for a few years before she was offered a full-time job. By then, she had a pretty good idea of what she was getting into. "Collectives can be really dangerous to the people in them—there's such a time and energy commitment," but as she explains below, that kind of commitment, and her growing children (her son left the house the year she joined NEFCO) had a lot to do with why she took the job:

> I wanted a pretty demanding job anyway because I was breaking away from the mother thing. It was time to forget about my children, and NEFCO is an excellent way to forget my kids. . . . It's a big transition when your children start leaving home. . . . I wanted something that's just as important as the kids.

She now runs, along with Joan, the grains department of

NEFCO, which supplies its member co-ops with dozens of different grains, nuts, some juices, dried fruit, peanut butter, spices, and more. Sharon, Joan, and some part-time workers share the duties of ordering, receiving, and distributing the food, doing all the paperwork that goes along with the food and controlling the inventory. She is part of the New England grain buyers, a consortium of cooperative grain buyers. In addition, Sharon has spent a lot of time in the last year trying to straighten out some problems with Fedco Trucking, which supplies the warehouse with much of its grain. This activity involved several weekends traveling to Maine to participate in long, difficult meetings.

COMMITMENT TO KEEPING THINGS RUNNING

No doubt, every business has plenty of work to be done, but at NEFCO, the things to be done are extremely *visible*.

Food comes into the warehouse via the dock where the trucks unload. Some are huge diesel tractor-trailers filled with rice from New York City or Vermont cheddar. Others are small vans with locally made peanut butter or cider.

If the food is not palletized (stacked onto flat pallets for transporting), then each bag of rice or bucket of peanut butter must be stacked onto a pallet first. This is usually done by several people—whoever is available in the warehouse— since it is hard on the back and is a natural occasion for the collaborative work that NEFCO favors.

One activity that is constantly going on, especially in the cheese department, is what is known as *putting up orders*. This involves taking the week's cheese order (or monthly grain order) for a co-op and loading each item from the cheese cooler onto a pallet. Each co-op may order from five to thirty different items and different amounts of each. Again, the job is usually done by a team. The workers put on hats and coats and spend several hours in the cooler putting up orders, walking among stacks of cheese, lifting forty-pound boxes of cheddar, etc. Finally, they take the pallet out of the cooler and onto the dock for the co-op to pick up.

Wednesday mornings are probably the most predictably busy time in the warehouse. A large number of co-ops come to pick up their orders of cheese and grains, and a work group must start at 6 A.M. to fill them. The cheese room is filled with people from the co-ops awaiting their orders and taking care of the paperwork. People are moving in and out of the cooler; carts and pallets are moving from the cooler to the docks. Things don't usually slow up until around 2 P.M.

There is also some produce going through the warehouse, particularly in the summer, when the warehouse serves as a coordinator for locally grown produce being sent to food co-ops in Boston. This often means that during the summer, trucks come into the warehouse at 9:00 P.M. with produce picked that day in western Massachusetts or another nearby region. It also means that Leo, who is in charge of local produce, and another person must be there to meet the truck and stay until 1:00 A.M. or so unloading a few hundred cases of lettuce, tomatoes, or even strawberries.

Now and then, a work team stops to take a break. Someone grabs some juice from the cooler, maybe some cheese that has been set aside for eating, and everyone has a brief snack. Often, the workers end up talking about how they are going to do the rest of the day's work, a sort of informal planning that is very common and necessary. It is the work that needs to be done, not a time clock or boss, that determines when their break ends. Someone starts to move, and they all agree: it's time to get back to work.

The kind of work to be done at NEFCO generates a recurring sense of miniature crisis: a need for everyone who is there to get in and shove. For example, as I watched two people loading cheese and oil into a truck on its way to the Maine co-ops, by pushing pallets up a metal ramp, the pallet started to slip back. One person yelled for some help, and two others who were nearby quickly came and helped push the pallet the rest of the way into the truck.

One of the co-op workers explained how the work to be done generates its own commitment and makes it hard to hang back from giving one's all:

> Staff behavior is definitely affected by the amount of work that is waiting. The work itself creates a commitment, and people are tied into making sure things are done right.
>
> For myself, I'd emphasize the idea of working with other people was what led me in the direction of being committed, but that I found commitment and responsibility really took hold of the job. . . . I really bought into being committed. I probably bought in too much.

PART-TIME AND VOLUNTEER WORKERS

There are actually three types of workers at NEFCO, representing different levels of involvement, full-time staff being the most involved. In addition to the staff, there are part-time workers and "volunteers." The volunteers are people working for their food co-ops as part of their obligation to NEFCO—a kind of membership dues paid in labor. NEFCO uses them mostly to fill in during heavy work periods. Frequently, there are no volunteers in the warehouse at all, but on heavy days, there may be four or five in the morning and another group in the afternoon. (There is a certain irony to the term *volunteer,* since for their labors they get access to cheap food, while full-time staff are working in an atmosphere of "volunteerism" where they are giving part of their life to the food co-op movement.)

Since volunteers work only a few hours a month at most, they usually don't take on responsibility or become proficient, but if someone decides to get more involved in the warehouse and wants a part-time job, he or she can work as a "part-timer." There are usually one or two part-timers working at the warehouse, out of a constantly changing pool of a half dozen or so. Part-timers are also used to fill in heavy work periods, but unlike volunteers, they have learned more about the warehouse and take on some responsibilities. They get paid an hourly wage slightly above the federal minimum.

The part-time workers are very much like the full-time workers in that they are committed to food co-ops and want to work in a pleasant environment. However, for one reason or another, most of the part-timers are not willing or able to make the strong commitment to NEFCO that is required of full-time workers. "Part-time work is a realistic commitment," one person said, implying that the commitment expected of full-time staff at NEFCO is unrealistically demanding, at least for her.

But part-timers would be quick to point out that this attitude does not mean that they are not committed to NEFCO. Some of the part-timers take a very active interest in running the warehouse, making decisions, and dealing with problems.

The regular use of part-time workers is not a totally accepted situation. For one thing, it has never been agreed upon that the warehouse should use part-time workers as a solution to understaffing. Why not replace three or four part-timers with two full-time staff members for less money? (Since salaried staff put in such long work weeks, part-timers end up with a higher hourly wage than full-time staff.) Others feel that part-timers are important to the warehouse because of their "fresh energy" and their ability to fill in as peak labor. One part-timer said she felt that they "soak up a lot of emotional tension" by talking with people about warehouse problems but not being so involved: "I think we're valuable here because we don't work so hard that we burn out. We're able to take on responsibility and willing to train replacements if we decide to leave." When the part-time workers presented a proposal for a work contract, including representation in the collective decisions, the staff accepted it, although they took months to decide to do so. Since then, part-timers have been taking on more responsibility in areas like bookkeeping and ordering, besides the physical work. They are quite happy about doing so.

There is clearly a strong element of volunteerism among staff of all kinds.

MIXING MOTIVES

Organizing work as a nonhierarchical, nonspecialized collective makes possible for the workers a highly valued diversity of experience that is not only that of shifting activities, but of shifting motives—skill building, personal sharing, and collective commitment on a political level and an institutional level. Furthermore, this collective way of working permits the various motives to be linked in practice. They depend on each other. There are strong reasons that the staff has shied away frc_a job specialization.

But mixed motives also sometimes conflict. When we look at the description that follows of Samuel's day, which has him coming to the NEFCO warehouse already drained from a day's worth of work as a produce buyer, it is clear that his specialization and skill acquisition are leading him out of the collective sharing he also values. Similarly, the emotional

ups and downs of the clique of the longest established workers directly affect the atmosphere of the warehouse:

> I think we're going through a period now of being
> too close. It seems now that we're having some tension.
> There didn't seem to be much heavy ego clashing be-
> fore, which has been a problem lately. . . . There are
> many factors, personal and work-related.
> There's a potential now for people to leave—it has
> to do with frustration, goals not being realized, a lack of
> cooperation that affects our sense of commitment and
> community.

But at the same time, it is clear that the informality and
fluidity of the working roles in the NEFCO collective make it
possible for all kinds of motives to come into play for any
given worker, and for the various work motives to combine in
various ways at various times.

The grains and cheese departments are on four-week
schedules. One week, they receive and collate the co-op orders, and the next week, they order the food from suppliers.
The third week, they receive the food and then distribute it to
the co-ops (cheese does a distribution every week). Thus,
each week means a somewhat different set of activities for
just about everyone, alternating between weeks of predominantly physical work and others of more telephoning and
paperwork.

Despite the monthly cycle, every day there are several
chores to be done—price lists to be made out, orders to be
made, oil to be poured, floors to be cleaned—and if a staff
person isn't doing that job, she or he is probably making sure
that it gets done by a part-timer or a co-op volunteer, as this
work is done by a combination of full-time workers, part-
timers, and volunteers.

For every piece of food that goes through the warehouse,
there are several kinds of paperwork: the ordering process,

collating, billing, posting the invoices, pricing the items, and keeping track of inventory. In most working institutions in the United States, such tasks would be treated as the specialized jobs of "administrators" and "clerical workers." At NEFCO, paperwork is not the exclusive domain of the bookkeepers. Just about everyone does some amount of paperwork. In ordering weeks, Joan, Sharon, and others spend large parts of the day on the telephone taking orders, and other days posting the orders and recording the invoices for each order in a book of accounts receivable for each co-op. This kind of work is generally more solitary, requiring long stretches of sitting at a desk working an adding machine or talking on the phone.

When Sharon or another worker moves from paperwork to manual labor, the shift does appears not as moving from a more "important" or "more skilled" kind of work to work of lower status, but as a welcome rest from the strain of decision making, and as the personal refreshment of taking part in a convivial activity.

Sharon, a few other people, and I spent several hours one morning moving pallets around in the warehouse to make room for some shipments coming in that afternoon. Many of the pallets moved were bottles of fruit juices, boxes of six stacked five high. The pallets were heavy, and it was hot down in the poorly ventilated warehouse. Afterward, Sharon explained to me that this was the first day in several that she had been able to work this way:

> I'm real glad to be doing this today; the past few days I've been doing a lot of executive-type decision-making without the right kind of information, scribbling down notes and talking on the phone with co-ops and storefronts.

She told me something about the price of cashews going up and trying to decide what kind of contract to sign with cashew dealers in Boston, and consulting the co-ops as to what they wanted:

> But anyway, I'm happy that all I have to do today is push around pallets.
>
> It's not that it's boring (the phone work); it's just too much. There's no time between one decision and the next to think about whether it was a good decison or not. . . . In a way, that's good. I've learned to make decisions without worrying about them.

This ability to make businesslike decisions is, as noted, one that Sharon acquired in middle life, and through working at NEFCO. It is important to her sense of self-esteem. But she, like others in the warehouse, seems to value the mixture of business work and physical labor.

As she says,

> I like the physical work for the exercise and so that I know what's happening in the warehouse. I find that if I can get into it, the physical work provides a rhythm of its own and a sense of urgency. I don't just want to do the buying; I want to help bring it in, and I'm happy when I can get the job done.
>
> . . . There's internal motivation all right, but there's also pressure from the work that has to be done.
>
> What I really want to do is get better at what I'm doing—inventory control, buying, etc.—and, in a few years, turn it over to somebody else.

The concepts of rhythm and urgency that are provided by the work are mentioned by several other workers. Sharon also refers to a "symbiosis" between the various kinds of work that together make the warehouse function.

In the case of another worker, Paula, it seems clear that a current very high level of commitment to working at NEFCO is linked to a number of extra activities with the co-op movement that she has come to take on, in connection with NEFCO.

Paula became interested in NEFCO through her involvement in food co-ops and her "attraction to their decision-making process." She started out doing volunteer work for the fledgling warehouse but shied away from joining the staff because of the requested two-year commitment: "It seemed like an awfully long time and I wanted to talk them down to eighteen months, but I eventually applied for the job." Having worked at NEFCO for more than three years, she now displays tremendous commitment to the business and especially to the continued growth of food cooperatives.

Just working at NEFCO usually means a commitment to co-ops, but Paula also has taken on several duties that are extensions of normal NEFCO functions. These "extras" include her frequent role of helping groups who come to NEFCO wanting to form new co-ops. She also serves on NEFCO's board and represents NEFCO at some regional conferences.

Most of the time that Paula spends on direct warehouse functions is rather routine, although requiring many difficult business decisions. As she says, "Extras give your job a sense of importance, and your job gives the extras a sense of importance."

Paula spends most of her time working in the cheese department, shipping and receiving various dairy products and doing a lot of paperwork, but she also helps out in other parts of the warehouse and puts a lot of time into decision-making efforts. She works very long hours and likes "having a sense of understanding the warehouse. Not much escapes me." As a result, she is one of the dominant figures at NEFCO. Paula is also a good example of someone who is committed to NEFCO as a healthy business organization. It is a commitment to getting the work done beneath all of the political connotations. She feels that the motivation to do work at NEFCO is similar to that in other situations—usually managerial—where people are held responsible for the general success of an enterprise.

Karen, the bookkeeper, also gets involved in regional co-op activities, spending a lot of time helping other co-ops on financial problems and being treasurer of a loan fund for New England co-ops. Karen talked about how she sees the relationship between extra activities and her job at NEFCO:

> On this job it's so hard to define your hours. It's a fine line between personal and co-op interests, and there are a lot of things I do that are related. With the loan fund, it's in the interest of the co-ops to have someone familiar with their finances on the bank's board. A lot of my involvement is because the co-ops aren't just our customers; what happens to them affects us.

NEFCO runs on a huge sense of camaraderie and depends on this sense of camaraderie rather than on formal chains of authority and task specialization for getting things done.

It is hard to tell whether this camaraderie is due to or in spite of the shared responsibilities of running NEFCO. Paula said she wished she could "put on a hat and say, 'Now I'm in this role,' then take it off and be people's friend." People who seem the closest in friendship frequently disagree the most at staff meetings. Yet, the joint participation in decision making does necessitate a lot of interdependence among the staff, and thus a lot of interaction. A few times a year, the staff have weekend retreats where they can talk about their lives, their jobs, and NEFCO without as much pressure to get work done or decisions made. But during a period when the collective was very divided about some decisions, several people expressed the feeling that the personal supportiveness of the staff was also breaking down. "We just aren't as close as we used to be. I miss it," Samuel said.

During times of great stress, the personal obligation created by friendship also helps keep people going. Being unable to do something means that another staff person, a friend perhaps, must get it done. For instance, Joan talked about this when she was considering leaving the staff:

>What makes it especially hard is that I feel like I am good friends with a lot of people here. It's not just a job; it's your friends that you're going through this with. If I left, I'd be leaving all of my responsibilities with Sharon, and I don't want to do that.

When Joan first started working at NEFCO, she said that she wanted a job that would be very personally involving for her, as "an extension of her life." Now she was having strong doubts about NEFCO and the level of involvement that she wanted in her job, feeling that it gets "dangerous if you don't keep your life balanced." She did end up leaving, partly because she felt the job was demanding too much of her life, in both time and emotional involvement.

The strong element of voluntarism within the NEFCO staff makes for a high input of energy and a strong sense of collegiality, but it can make trouble as well, particularly when some people see as proper a higher level of commitment than others do, and they pressure the others to come along.

Consistent with her commitment to the business, Paula is known for her frugality with staff expenses. She has always pushed for keeping staff salaries low and expecting the present staff to take on additional work loads during heavy periods:

>I think that we would double or quadruple our staff costs to move the same volume of food if we staffed so no one would ever have to take on extra tasks. I don't feel anyone should be forced to do something they don't want to do, but I don't think you find salaried people in society working a set number of hours.

While no one wants staff costs to quadruple, other people do want to see forty-hour weeks and, in some cases, better pay. "I think that after we've had a few real heavy weeks, we should be able to have a light week," Sharon once said. Some people feel that Paula expects them to commit the same amount of their life to NEFCO and resent the pressure as "guilt tripping." Out of concern for her health as well as their own needs, Paula has been twice requested by the rest of the staff to reduce her hours.

One person at the warehouse pointed out that the highly personalized atmosphere at NEFCO makes a person feel very important to the organization. In addition, loose job roles allow people to be involved in many aspects of the warehouse, and as a result, "The individual plays such an important part in the collective, that you are difficult to replace."

When I asked Paula when she might consider leaving, she said,

> That's the problem; I have no idea when to leave. There isn't any agreement about what these jobs are, if they are careers for big chunks of life, specialized jobs in the co-op movement, or whether they should be shared around. Theoretically, sharing the jobs sounds good, but it doesn't feel like the job I've been doing. Others could have done it, but it wasn't easy.

Paula, along with each person on the staff, has carved herself a unique place in both the work load and the personal environment at NEFCO, and the responsibility inherent in that niche is one of the things that keeps her there.

TURNOVER AND JOB CAREERS

In its first few years, NEFCO had an extremely high staff turnover. No one stayed at the job for more than two years, and many left before working a year. At one point, virtually the whole staff left and a new group replaced them; it was at this point that NEFCO began asking for a minimum two-year commitment. A core group developed, several of whom have now been at the warehouse more than three years.

Along with this core group and the two-year commitment, there was the beginning of a change in attitude toward NEFCO jobs. Previously, the jobs were not considered permanent occupations at all, but temporary jobs in the co-op movement. The people were younger and were often interested in other employment. In contrast, the core group were older and more capable of commiting a few years of their life—Sharon was coming out of child rearing, Sam had many years of food business experience, Karen had already been a bookkeeper for many years—even though they still may not have considered the job a long-term career. They also had some long-range goals for the warehouse and themselves, such as Sharon's wanting to develop business skills, or Samuel's desire to see produce go through the warehouse. For these people, NEFCO was more than just a transient co-op job and an entry-level business position right from the start.

All this is not to say that there isn't turnover at NEFCO. One person recently left before his two-year commitment ended, and two people have been fired in the last several years. Gradually, some of the more long-term workers are leaving as well, although they have stayed involved in local co-op activities. But turnover has been reduced as the staff has grown into a supportive group, seeking commitment and developing individual skills.

SAMUEL'S WORKING DAY: PRODUCE BUYING AS POLITICAL ACTION

For Samuel, NEFCO has provided a marvelously appropriate way of bringing the skills he learned as the child of small-grocery owners into the context of the political interests he acquired while growing up. He joined NEFCO to be part of "a community cooperative working to obtain some goals . . . an experiment in how people are going to eventually make decisions." But the specialized work he does for NEFCO takes him out of the warehouse for most of the day, away from the sorting, loading, and hauling that welds most of the staff into a group. For him, it has been particularly important to have been part of a group decision-making process at meetings of the collective in which the political meaning of the work can be made explicit.

Samuel's experience working with food began with his family's "mom and pop" store in Boston. He worked in the store before going to college and eventually ran the store after his father become ill. Between the store and a day-care job, he was often putting in eighty-hour work weeks. Then, in 1974, the store was finally sold, and he quit his day-care job and began his involvement with food cooperatives. He became the representative for his local co-op to the fledgling New England Food Cooperative and was part of their search for a new warehouse. From there, he "just sort of drifted into it," becoming a part-time produce buyer and getting more involved in daily staff operations. There was no formal hiring process, but he became the full-time produce buyer when the position was vacated.

Sam had dabbled in "alternative things" in the past, so there was a certain logic in his food and business experience leading him into the food cooperative movement of the mid-1970s. He had worked for a crisis hot line and had volunteered at a community high school before focusing on co-ops: "My involvement was a gradual progression. I liked being in the association of people working together, breaking down some of the authoritative things. . . . People on the staff were generally a very warm group of people, easy to get along with."

The decision-making processes of NEFCO, a cooperative and a collective, were very important to Sam's initial interest in his job there. He saw the collective as a means of workplace control, and the cooperative as a means of broader community control over food distribution.

Sam is one of two full-time produce buyers. They collate individual co-op orders and then buy in large quantities at Chelsea market three mornings a week. Many co-ops in the NEFCO federation are too small to buy at Chelsea, so buying collectively allows them access to a higher level of food distribution. In addition, NEFCO buyers such as Sam are there several days a week, becoming consistent buyers for the co-ops. This approach is more effective than a rotating or voluntary system, which would be necessary if no permanent produce buyers existed.

Produce buying at NEFCO operates on a weekly cycle. Sam usually spends Mondays making phone calls to the market and looking over his own information in order to make weekly projections of prices and the availability of items. In the afternoon, he conveys that information to some of the co-ops as they begin to call in their orders for the next day: "A lot of the co-ops want to know the conditions on the market . . . prices and stuff . . . before they buy some items or so they know how much they want. . . . A lot of work goes into it."

He also does this work on Mondays to make the rest of his week a little easier. By calling around on Monday, he knows what is going to be hard to find and where he might get it at a good price: "It's sort of like being in second gear on Tuesday, when I go to the market. If I didn't make calls on Monday, I'd have to be in first gear to get things done."

On a Tuesday morning, Sam and Karen arrive at the market at 4:30 A.M. The sun won't rise for almost two hours, but the market is already bustling. There is a constant flow of diesel trailer trucks in and out of the main gate. The sound of the trucks and the smell of diesel exhaust are everywhere. Inside the main gate are four long warehouses with a loading dock and room for fifty or sixty of the huge trailer-trucks to back up to it on either side. Most of the bays are full, the trucks fanning out from the warehouses like giant arms.

Inside the first warehouse is a large display area with boxes of each item opened and neatly displayed. There is an area with dozens of different citrus fruits, and after that the vegetables. The center serves as a kind of causeway where people are talking and moving about. Others are clustered around the booths where the order cards and receipts are made out.

Sam walks into this melee armed only with a piece of paper on which are written the items he will buy and the amount ordered by each co-op. Because he has made phone calls to the market the previous day, the first area he goes to is where he thinks he can get items in short supply. As he walks up to a cluster of people, a man immediately puts an arm around Sam's shoulder, leading him toward a stack of crates: "Listen, Sammy, I've been saving these beans for you 'cause I know you buy from me every day. The market's real short on 'em today, Sammy."

Sam seems in a hurry and not all that interested in what the man has. He walks over to some of the crates and opens them, reaching down and bringing up an eggplant from the bottom, turning it around and squeezing it. He does the same for a case of zucchini, sifting through the box to pull out the ones from the bottom.

"No everyone, but some of these guys will pick out the right sizes and shapes for the display boxes. These guys here aren't too bad, though," he tells me.

"Sammy, all that stuff's new, that Texas load," yells the man from across the aisle. We walk over to inspect the Texas produce, and Sam points out that the leeks aren't really from Texas. "The greens have been chopped; they got frost somehow so they're probably from New Jersey or around there. I'll show you some Texas leeks later," he tells me. Sam clearly takes pride in his knowledge of the market.

Eventually, he buys a few items at this first warehouse: eggplant and beans, which he knows he won't be able to get elsewhere.

In the next few hours, Sam and I walk around the market going into several of the houses. (A "house" is a section of the warehouse, and each is filled by a different distributing company.) Rather than moving from one contiguous house to another, we move randomly among a half dozen houses that are spread through the whole market, returning to some of them two or three times. In each of the houses we visit, the people know Sam on a first-name basis. These people see each other nearly every day, and there is a strong sense of daily routine in their rapport. There are nicknames and little idiosyncracies in the way each person or each house treats Samuel, and vice versa. Some people keep their heads down as they write orders into books while others chat first. They often don't exchange formal greetings; instead, they fall immediately into a discussion about some produce items:

"Ah, my dear Samuel, have I got a beautiful cuke for you."

"You got any peppers? That's what I need."

"I need a whole pallet today."

"You got it, pal, you got it."

The talk is friendly, but the prevailing atmosphere of the market is clear. As Karen said, "In spite of the camaraderie and bullshit that goes on, it is a business relationship."

Sam might walk into a group of people who are standing around and join in some joking small talk. Then, he'll go to the back of the warehouse and open a few cases of each item to check their quality with that of the displays in front. Before he leaves, he'll get the prices on the items he's interested in.

Sam and the seller, each with pad in hand, exchange a

flurry of words and numbers, mostly unintelligible to me but easily understood by them. Sam jots a few things down and says he's not sure what he wants right now and leaves. Sam explains to me that for some of the people he deals with, he'll actually buy the items first and then negotiate the price later over the phone. He knows what price he'll get from them, so he buys early to be sure the items are available. Storage items, like potatoes, have a very stable price: "He gives me the same price all the time. He'll try to give me a week's notice if the price is gonna go up" (so Sam can buy while they're cheaper).

In some ways, Sam leads a double life at the market. The first half of the morning he spends with people who have worked at Chelsea for most of their lives, many having entered the market through traditional family ties. In the latter half of the day, he deals mostly with co-op workers, of whom even the regulars are relative newcomers to the market and could be regarded as outsiders. Sam has integrated himself extremely well into both worlds. His job demands such integration, since he is a vital link between the co-ops and the produce market.

Visually, Sam looks more like the usual market worker than a co-op worker. His hair is cut short, and he wears a black nylon coat with his name on the pocket. It is the uniform of the produce worker, the same type of coat worn by nearly everyone in the market.

Produce sellers know that Samuel is buying for the co-ops, and they see him and Karen as representatives of the co-ops. One morning when I was there, several people commented to Sam about a newspaper article on food co-ops in which Sam was interviewed. Another time, he got into a discussion about co-op buying policies in regard to chemicals used that are detrimental to farmworkers.

After an hour of buying, Sam goes to Prince Tomato

Company, where he has arranged to meet with drivers for
two co-ops that haven't put in their order yet. Sam advises
them on the prices of some items. Beans are too expensive,
broccoli's not good either. Pineapples might be nice, but wait
a week on the asparagus . . . maybe a bargain on artichokes.
"The eggplant's getting expensive now, they're higher than
they were but not too expensive yet." The woman orders
some eggplant, so Sam has to call another warehouse to get
it: "Leo, I'm gonna get one more eggplant. Can you write up
a cash ticket for Buckport co-op?"

Around 6:30 A.M., Sam and Karen meet with the other
co-op people at Prince Tomato. As soon as he walks in, he
gets a phone call from Paula at NEFCO. Then, he and Karen
start going through their orders and writing out tickets for
individual co-ops. Drivers for the co-ops are starting to show
up, and by 7:30, there are fifteen people at Prince Tomato
sorting through their tickets. The tickets tell the driver the
location, price, and quantity of each item to pick up.

The next few hours are what Sam calls "assorted crazi-
ness": dealing with late orders, mistakes, and trucking arrangements. He talks with all of the drivers as they come in.
He makes some phone calls to get final prices on some items.

Then he spends some time doing "splits," where two
smaller co-ops will split a case of peppers or a bag of carrots.
Sam makes sure that the money works out correctly and
sometimes divides the orders up himself. One of the co-op's
trucks has broken down, so Sam arranges for another co-op
to deliver its produce.

From Chelsea, the trucks go to the NEFCO warehouse,
where they pick up citrus fruits and cheeses, and Sam coordi-
nates them so they don't all arrive there at once, to make it
easier on the warehouse workers.

Tuesdays are particularly heavy, even with a head start
by telephoning on Monday. Sam mentioned that even

though we were moving quickly, it still wasn't until 6:30 that he was able to sit down to collect his thoughts and begin to write out tickets. One morning, Sam disappeared for more than an hour and came back looking quite haggard. He had been arguing with a distributor—trying to get a refund for what a co-op claimed was an overcharge—and had finally succeeded. "You just have to be insistent. If you're right about something you got to stick to it . . . eventually they'll respect you on it," he said afterward.

Somewhere around 9:30, the co-ops have all been taken care of, and it is time to drive back to NEFCO. For most people, the day is just beginning, but Sam and Karen's day is six hours old. In that period, they have made an enormous number of decisions and arrangements, so that by the time he leaves the market, Sam is visibly more nervous and high-strung: "From four o'clock, when you get up, you start gearing your head up for dealing with the issues of the day, making the decisions and things." Karen, who is still learning the job, finds that it demands long periods of concentrating, making quick decisions, and bearing the responsibility. It is after this kind of stressful activity that Sam and Karen return to the warehouse three mornings each week.

In addition to buying produce for co-ops at Chelsea, NEFCO also buys produce itself, brings it to the warehouse, and then resells it to co-ops as they come to pick up grains and cheese. Much of Sam's work at the warehouse is dealing with this produce, as well as physically moving it through the warehouse. The use of NEFCO as a produce brokerage developed largely through Sam's initiative. As it turned out, it required major changes in his workday that have now become a permanent part of his job.

Samuel did not always spend much time working at the warehouse. In his first year as a produce buyer, he worked almost exclusively at the Chelsea market and had very little involvement with the warehouse. At that time, there were no regular staff meetings, which would have brought Sam more frequently into the warehouse. He was mostly in the warehouse to take orders over the phone. That winter, he thought it would be more convenient if NEFCO would market citrus fruit through the warehouse, rather than requiring co-ops to pick it up at Chelsea. This procedure would have made the fruits available to many co-ops that couldn't previously purchase them. The workers at the warehouse, however, felt that there was no room in the cooler for the fruit and that they couldn't handle the extra work. This decision prompted Sam to spend more time in the warehouse so that he could understand what was going on and eventually help get the citrus fruit going through.

After that proved successful, they began bringing some storage items through the warehouse, like potatoes, squash, and avocados. Finally, they have begun to bring "weird" items through the warehouse, like chestnuts, dill, fennel, and kohlrabi. These are items that even large co-ops can use in only small amounts, so buying them through the warehouse allows several co-ops to split a case.

Although it only developed recently, this function of NEFCO has been in Sam's mind almost since he first began as a produce buyer. He saw the problems that Chelsea created for co-ops and thought NEFCO could provide an alternative. One of his goals is to see NEFCO do all of the produce in this way, as a brokerage. He sees it as something to accomplish before leaving his NEFCO job.

Once in the warehouse, Sam didn't limit himself to working on produce. He started helping in the cheese cooler doing some bookkeeping and pricing, particularly when staffing was short. Apparently, time spent in the warehouse

was important enough for him to expand his hours. One
result was fifty- or sixty-hour work weeks, but he also received some definite rewards:

> . . . What is it that motivates someone to go crazy
> for a couple of years busting your ass in a collective
> warehouse? It certainly isn't the tangible things like
> money or spare time. I think it has to be those intangible
> things. The benefits here are the people you work with.

These "personal benefits" are particularly true of his relationship with three other staff members, the four of them
forming a sort of "old-timer" clique. Along with a fifth person, they have all worked at NEFCO for more than three years.

Another result of Sam's increased amount of warehouse
work was his increased participation in warehouse decision-
making. When Sam started on citrus fruit in the warehouse,
there were no regular meetings that included all of the staff.

He began to push for regular staff meetings ("I don't
think people in the warehouse did much to bring produce
people into the collective"), and regular meetings were a way
of connecting produce with the warehouse operations: "I'm
always the one who gets pissed when a meeting gets can-
celed. . . . I don't like them either, but I think they're necessary." A year and a half later, Sam was also the initiator of a
new meeting structure designed to make the staff decision
process more effective and less time-consuming, problems
that were becoming more severe as the staff grew. While
everyone recognized the need for such a structure, it was
Sam who presented a detailed proposal and talked it through
at a meeting.

Sam has also developed one of the more articulate phi-
losophies about the collective process at NEFCO, as he re-
vealed in one discussion:

> Work toward being a collective, that's our biggest
> problem. Different people have different ideas of what

that means. People pull back from it because it's frustrating. I think people have a fear of the collective process.
It's not a debate; it's more a Hegelian process. All those
theses come into the pot and a new thing comes out. It's
rare that my initial decision is what the collective decision turns out to be.

People have to have the room to express their
views, and then listen to others' views. . . . Then you
end up having a group process.

He is not always able to execute those ideas in his own
behavior. Other workers have complained that Sam is difficult to approach and is often irritable, although they write it
off as due to intense job pressures. He is apt to get angry at
meetings and has even walked out. At the same time, Sam
also frequently takes a mediator role at meetings, summariz-
ing arguments, proposing alternatives, and sometimes inject-
ing bits of philosophy about the collective process to make all
the frustration seem a little more worthwhile ("We're experimenting with our lives in trying to work in collectives. We
have so few role models, so few things in our upbringing").
He is also looked to for advice on some business matters since
he is the most experienced in business.

During a meeting to discuss two applicants for a bookkeeping position, Sam received an urgent phone call from
Rhode Island telling him that his father was extremely ill. He
had been expecting the phone call and knew that he had to
leave immediately, but the timing was terrible. The workers
all agreed, including Sam, that the hiring decision could not
be delayed, even if it meant his exclusion from the process.
Sam was visibly upset, pacing back and forth, obviously torn
between the necessity to see his family and his desire to be in
on the decision:

I feel uncomfortable about leaving because I think
we're going to have trouble reaching consensus on

> this. . . . I am more concerned about leaving that prob-
> lem than about who's hired out of the three.

The difficulty was resolved by having Sam call from his family's house to see how the meeting was going.

Making the decision, as it turned out, was easier than
expected, and consensus was reached, although most people
expressed surprise at the outcome. Several days later, Sam
told me that he was not sure what his choice would have
been, but he thought the decision was a very good one:

> The collective as a whole is responsible for running
> the business, that's how I operate. . . . What bothers me
> about the staff hiring is that I didn't have a chance to
> disagree.

MAJOR PROBLEMS AND CONFLICTS

During the period I spent working with the NEFCO staff,
there was often an atmosphere of chaos, conflict, and over-
work. There were several major ongoing decisions (such as
whether to go into the trucking business), a few simmering
personality conflicts, and a shortage of space and of labor
power, all of which added to the work load and reduced
efficiency. More bothersome, however, was the "crisis-to-
crisis" feeling that the organization sometimes took on. Although the crises were certainly affected by personality conflicts and major decisions in the works, there were some
greater organizational problems that everyone could feel.

A major underlying factor in these problems was the
rapid growth of the warehouse over a period of a few years.
Volume and functions had increased, and along with these
increases, the staff size had nearly tripled in three years. This
growth had had an impact on the functioning of NEFCO in
two main ways. The growth made many of the previous ways

of working impractical and awkward. For instance, loose cash-flow and bookkeeping procedures became a mess, making auditing and planning difficult; full staff meetings grew from five to twelve people and would drag on for hours without decisions.

In addition, the rapid growth in staff size created some schisms in the collective. Newer members came in with different priorities for organizing the warehouse and their jobs. Although conflicts did not always fall along new and old staff lines, it seemed that the "old guard" sought to defend the existing organization of the warehouse and their roles in it, while newer members, with less at stake, wanted it changed to suit their own needs.

These conflicts and problems resulting from growth generated a lot of discussion about what it is like, or should be like, to work at NEFCO. The way in which the problems were dealt with was, unfortunately, not always so easy to observe or understand. Nevertheless, the conflicts did bring out several main issues of job satisfaction and motivation for many workers in the warehouse.

LOOSE JOB ROLES VERSUS DEFINED RESPONSIBILITY

As the staff grew and warehouse problems became more complex, more workers began complaining about the seeming lack of control over their work and the unclear definition of their responsibilities.

Earlier members had enjoyed rather loose job roles, partly because these functioned better for them. There was also a general philosophy of nebulous job descriptions and roles' allowing a person more freedom to shape her or his own job without the constraints of a defined role. This approach would reduce monotony while also preventing one person from taking control over one area, since many people are involved in each activity.

Early staffers arranged their jobs according to this philosophy as much as possible. They had, however, inherited the warehouse organized along departmental lines; "produce," "grains," "cheese," and bookkeeping. Some workers found this organization undesirable since it caused people to be in more set roles ("produce worker," "grains worker," etc.), and they sought to gradually get rid of them. "Despite all our attempts to the contrary, those departments are still with us," the bookkeeper said at a hiring interview. In fact, a few people were hired as "general warehouse workers," although it was clear where they were needed.

Other warehouses where workers were most strictly divided in jobs were looked down on. After visiting a food warehouse in New York, Paula noted that there were people who strictly did books and didn't get out of the office. Other people were just on the docks, shipping and receiving. "They all seemed kind of bored in the routine of their jobs. . . . I think we're nice in the unusual way that we [NEFCO] are."

The desire to abolish departments did leave the position of bookkeeper intact, as a somewhat necessary evil, an acknowledged position of power. However, Karen saw it as an important goal in her job to make the bookkeeping system understandable and accessible, with several people involved in it and capable of running it. The major point was to ensure that the organization would not be dependent on her to run the finances. This idea of not having the organization depend on any one worker (as a point of power) was common and seemed to go along with the nebulous-job-roles principle. The books were accessible, and several people did share many bookkeeping tasks, but they were also quite confused.

Many of the problems at the warehouse, however, began to point to the loose job roles and responsibilities. There was a general feeling that things were very difficult to control, and many small things were not getting done because no one knew who should do them. There was a sense that the organization was "an oversized monster, with a lot of steam roller to it, big and hard to change." Lack of defined responsibility made it hard to get control of the organization's functioning. One person said she felt that "everyone is made responsible for the whole thing while no one is responsible for one thing."

It also became clear that some people were feeling less in control than others. One person seemed to be "running" the cheese department by virtue of putting in more hours than anyone else. Samuel was criticized for effectively controlling the produce department because he held so much information in his head (prices, orders, etc.) and there was no procedure for sharing it. After being on the job for six months, a new produce buyer said she still felt "sort of like a little sister tagging along."

A desire for more clearly defined jobs became stronger. A "general warehouse worker" asked for a more specific description of her job and duties. The staff began conducting "job reviews" in which one person discussed his or her job and how it might be changed. At one point, the staff decided to have everyone write a detailed description of all the jobs he or she was doing, "so we can see what we are doing and decide what we can and can't do."

Much of this runs against the nebulous job-role idea. As Sharon said, "There's an ideological feeling against specialization that I don't share. . . . I think it's bad if it's so narrow that you don't know what else is going on, but it doesn't have to be"—and later, "What I really want to do is get better at what I'm doing—inventory control, buying—and in a few years turn it over to someone else."

Conflicts around job definitions came out clearly around

the notion of warehouse "reorganization," a term that floated around as something they always wanted to get around to doing. Some people were more anxious to see reorganization than others, particularly those who felt more frustrated and less in control.

Everyone seemed to have different ideas of what *reorganization* meant. Some felt the solution was in continuing toward abolishing the departments and carving out new jobs in a departmentless place. Others made a push for strengthening the departments as they were. Concrete proposals were scarce, but one came up for the cheese department that involved creating tightly defined roles within the department and rotating them among the people who worked in the department: "It would be a situation where you could know what you're doing and know someone else is doing what other jobs need doing." The idea was never fully considered, perhaps because it was not decided that departments should exist, but also because its formalized power-sharing was threatening to some.

While the conflicts sometimes seemed like a struggle between particular people's opinions, the struggle was also an ideological struggle between the values of loose job roles and the desire to have control over one's own area, a struggle felt by all. As the need for reorganization became more clear, so did the need for better job definition and control. Old ways of doing things, lack of communication, concentration of power, and personal problems all seemed to be in the way of a desire to get control of things: "If we could get through this childlishness, then we could get on with controlling the work."

Paula, previously one of the strongest supporters of loose job structure and abolishing departments, also saw the need for increased job specification. She laid out the situation very well:

I think that before having a large staff, we have to have kind of strict rules about what is staff; we have to define what responsibilities we share, who shares them and in what way. When it was smaller, there was less need to do that, and it was less important. In the older staff, there had been instead of setting down a strict set of rules, a sort of sloppy way of looking at it—"This is what staff does"—but it was also a way of putting things on a personal level.

PROBLEMS WITH DECISION MAKING

NEFCO is officially run by a democratic decision-making process that is highly valued by the staff. They are, however, aware that consensus decision-making is easier said than done, as people's commitment is strained during long, frustrating meetings and disturbing power struggles. Still, an enormous amount of time and effort is put into the decision process, often more than is warranted by the actual changes in job structure that result. For instance, formalizing the position of part-time workers in the warehouse took many hours of meetings and discussion, yet resulted in few actual changes in how the work gets done. Workers participate in the decision process partly out of a commitment to the process itself, as a highly desirable political goal and as essential to the continued functioning of NEFCO. Thus, creating a voice for part-time workers in staff decision-making was consistant with a desire to see people participate in their workplace, even though it added another person to the already-crowded staff meetings.

As the staff grew larger, NEFCO's decision making problems also grew. Full staff meetings, where major decisions were to be made, were long, frustrating, and unproductive. Important business decisions, such as rescheduling truck runs and reorganizing office space, were not being made. Sometimes, it was unclear if a decision had been arrived at or not. At one meeting, someone announced that he had found a small truck to buy but was still not sure if they had decided to buy a truck or not, even though they had supposedly decided at the last meeting.

The size of meetings wasn't the only barrier to smooth decisions. It was also apparent that some members had considerably more power than others, despite ideals to the contrary. Examples of this kind of power were hard to observe, but it seemed clear that the three people who had been there the longest exerted a lot of influence and that much of this power came out of the large amount of hours that each of these people worked. Paula spent enough time in the warehouse so that she had something to do with nearly everything. While she regarded this involvement as important for understanding the warehouse, others regarded it as a form of control. Karen, the bookkeeper, controlled the departments' buying policy by managing cash flows. Samuel, besides being dominant in the produce department, was frequently consulted by others on business matters. To the extent that they relied on him, he gained power. "There is some power in the jobs with the most pressing business decisions. That's an issue that hasn't been dealt with," Paula once noted.

Individual personalities—how easily people worked with others on decisions—played a big part in these struggles. Paula described her own situation:

> Being in a collective was definitely a different amount of work for me than for other people. . . . A lot of people's style would be to quickly talk to people about, well, how many cases of crackers should we get four weeks from now, and my personal style of just knowing how many we need without talking to anybody, that's a problem. I view it as a personality thing. People have said that it's not OK to know how many

crackers to get four weeks from now, and even if you know, you have to make the appearance of asking people.

Another person described how style enters into meetings:

Some people are willing to get mad, and the person who yells the loudest gets power. A lot of decisions end up being made by other people giving up.

Joan related many of the decision problems to problems of structurelessness:

Our basic problem is that we said we have a decision-making structure but we don't. We cling to the ideal consensus decision but it hasn't worked for us. We don't make decisions by consensus. . . . A lot of us have felt that people have unfairly used this position of being rather structureless. Some people have gotten a lot more power than others, and there is no way of approaching that and saying, "No, that isn't acceptable."

Sharon also felt frustrated by a lack of structure for solving problems:

I knew there were problems, but I thought the structure was set up to solve them together. . . . Eventually I felt like I was bumping my head against a plate glass window. . . . If we could just get through some of this childishness, we could get on with controlling the work.

The frustrations that staff people felt were heightened by the high level of commitment that people felt to running the business and working toward a smooth decision process. Feeling a lot of anger and frustration, people would still work at solutions by arranging more meetings or extending the regular ones. High commitment meant that many people were personally involved in whatever was being decided, adding to the difficulty of making decisions:

It's rare that we can sit down and make a decision on a specific issue. You're making decisions on a person's life, and they have a lot of implications. If you are committed to running NEFCO well, then any decision is personally involving, not just for you but for ten other people on the staff as well.

CONCLUSION

What sets NEFCO apart from other warehouses, or most hourly wage jobs, is the workers' commitment to their work: commitment to each other, to the business, to food co-ops, or to political change. There are elements of each in all of the staff members. Some of the enviable characteristics of NEFCO—financial stability and growth, worker management, and lowered turnover—are directly related to this level of staff commitment. But how unique to the NEFCO situation is their commitment? Would it be possible to have a staff so committed to their work if the warehouse were not an important part of the food cooperative movement? If people are so motivated by a sense of political change, then it is unlikely that they would be as involved in a job that did not have that connection?

Samuel spends a lot of time helping co-ops decide what kinds of produce to buy based on his knowledge of the market, and he has put a lot of work into making it easier for small co-ops to get produce through the warehouse. Would Samuel still be so concerned about his customers if he were buying produce for grocery stores? Would Paula be motivated to work so many hours if there were not an interplay between her job and her "extra" interests in the national co-op movement?

The answer is probably not, but not necessarily "no." The

social change context of NEFCO is unique, but it is not the only motivation, and on a daily basis, others seem more important. For instance, when Len says, "It's not like you're working for someone else and they are worrying about these things and you punch out at five o'clock," the important thing is that he is working for himself and that is why he works so hard. Commitment inspired by participation in the organization and collective responsibility is not to be underestimated. A tremendous amount of energy is put into collective management above the usual work duties. Participating in decisions also affects the staff's commitment to the rest of their work: "It's not just that we are working collectively; it's also collective responsibility for running the business." The collective's self-management is probably the most essential part of the staff's high motivation, and while it still carries a political aspect, it is not unique to food cooperative warehouses.

Finally, the aspect of the warehouse that is most removed from politics is the personal environment. The atmosphere of friendship and support has reduced staff turnover and allowed strong commitments to the business to grow. Relying on each other for group decisions, physical help, and moral support is what really holds the place together. But again, just as commitment to the business stems from participation in decisions, so are personal obligation and support inextricably tied to shared responsibility in decision making and mutual reliance.

Chapter 7

EVERYBODY WORKS
Sheltered Work

WITH PETER LINKOW AND SHARON MORIEARTY

Work is a social category. The activities that people call their work, whatever they are in themselves and to the individual, have a special dimension because they are framed as the exchange that the worker makes with society. To be working legitimizes the worker as a social being.

Thus, we create work roles for those we want to tie into society: juvenile delinquents, the disabled, the mentally retarded. Sheltered workshops for such people are work settings the primary purpose of which is therapeutic. The sheltered workshop we describe here is for the mentally retarded. It is a setting in which the framing of activity as work is absolutely central. It is, in fact, *the* point of it all. The work is not interesting. It is not particularly valuable, either in monetary terms or in any other way. The pay is trifling. The workers can exercise practically no initiative in structuring their own labor. But the satisfaction of being a worker is substantial.

The modern industry of sheltered work owes its immediate economic heritage to the federal employment programs of the New Deal. Along with the CCC and the WPA came the RSA, or Rehabilitation Services Administration. The mandate of the new agency was to subsidize a work experience for those adults who could not be "absorbed" into the competitive labor market.

Today, the RSA is in charge of a basic state grant program of approximately $900 million annually, which funds a variety of vocational rehabilitation services purchased by the states from their local private institutions. Chief among these purchased services is the "sheltered workshop," a predominantly nonprofit form of middleman operation that marries marginal labor to marginal work, the social worker to the entrepreneur.

In Massachusetts, the scene of our investigation, there are approximately 160 privately owned workshop sites across the state, with a combined daily attendance of 6,300 persons. These facilities range in size from a labor force of less than 30 to over 100. Over one-third of these enterprises have been in operation for at least ten years, though the average net return on investment is around 3 percent per annum, and deficit budgets are not uncommon.

The primary source of labor for a workshop today is referral from a government agency. Programs like those sponsored by the RSA pay a workshop a daily rate for each individual "client" it refers to the setting. These rates vary depending on the type of work training experience requested for a client, though as a practical matter, there is very little variation in the kinds of job experiences workshops can or do offer. Workshops also solicit labor through private referrals from the local community, in which case a tuition rate is applied. Fees and tuitions tend to comprise the major portion of workshop gross receipts, followed by subcontract income.

Private industries are attracted into contracts with sheltered workshops for various kinds of portable, unskilled labor, generally labor-intensive jobs that may be unprofitable if performed on site at negotiated wage rates. A classic example is a recycling job, where an industry wants to reclaim its raw materials, and the necessary automated salvage technology does not exist. Industries may also recognize a charitable purpose in a subcontract award. In addition, the federal government and, today, most states have enacted preferential statutes for the awarding of certain nontechnical, labor-intensive government contracts to sheltered workshops. And finally, workshops canvas for subcontracts from local eleemosynary institutions, such as a church in need of centerpieces for a pot luck or a policeman's benevolent association seeking the duplication of brochures for the annual ball. Industries and charitable groups tend to impute a public interest to steering work toward a sheltered workshop and often reason backward to adapt a job need to that labor and the setting.

In some workshops, the U.S. Department of Labor sets a base wage at half the mandated minimum. However, a setting classified as a "work activity center" may set wages on a fluctuating productivity margin below even this level.

The workshop's split personality as social work agency on the one hand and subcontractor on the other makes for uncertainties in the flow of work and labor. The classic assembly-line organization of most workshop enterprises has as much to do with these market parameters as with the unique nature of the work force itself.

RIVER WORKSHOP

One of these sheltered workshops for the retarded is River Workshop, part of River Association for Retarded Cit-

izens, a nonprofit voluntary organization founded in the early 1950s by parents of retarded children. The ARC, as it is
known, is a charter member of a grass-roots affiliate movement that began to take shape on a national scale shortly
following World War II. The founding impetus was two-fold:
to provide a supportive social community for matters traditionally not discussed outside the home, and to piece together a cooperative, family-centered system of services for
retarded children, whose opportunities for care and treatment at that time were limited to remote institutional
placement.

River Association grew up with its children. The early
programs, staffed by parents on a time-sharing basis, concentrated on childhood needs, family therapies, and pre-
academic curricula. As the children matured, new programs
were created to prepare them for productive adult roles.

River Association, like many of its sister ARCs, received
a major stimulus for its initiative during the early 1970s when
state and federal governments began to show an interest in
developing community-based alternatives to the controversial institutional systems.

Today, River Association is a $1-million-a-year enter-
prise, offering a variety of day training and more limited residential programs for retarded adults and some children.
Doing business with the state has been a losing proposition
since the beginning, necessitating chronic fundraisers to
make up a contract deficit, but one enterprise pays its way
and even yields a modest return to keep the others afloat.
This is the sheltered workshop.

The workshop community is situated on three acres of
pleasant woodland nestled atop a hill overlooking the old
colonial center of a Boston suburb. The only marking as one
leaves the main road to begin a slow circular climb to the
summit is a small hewn-wood sign announcing "River Association for Retarded Citizens."As guests leave from behind

the birches that line the road, they are greeted by three one-story concrete structures of distinctly military heritage. These three utilitarian structures are among the last vestiges of this site's use as a Nike base, outmoded by strategic jets and missiles.

Approximately a hundred mentally retarded men and women are employed in the various workshop enterprises carried on in these three buildings, one of which also contains the administrative offices. "Clients," as workshop employees are called, are drawn from surrounding communities, where they reside with families or in a variety of sheltered residential arrangements, such as public institutions, nursing homes, and what are commonly called *halfway houses.*

For approximately twenty-four members of the work force, the workshop community is also home. "Up the hill" a few hundred yards from the production sites are three modern and impressively commodious brick homes, each surrounded by a carefully manicured lawn. They have names: Mountain House, Stott House, and Salamone House.

PAY DAY

We arrive on a seductive midspring afternoon. This is payday, a biweekly event at River, and a social as well as economic event. One of the work supervisors has set up a card table just outside the entrance to the main workshop, from which he is distributing small manila envelopes. A number of workers have gathered for the occasion as the names of the recipients are read off in alphabetical order. The atmosphere is light and jovial, and a few jests can be overheard concerning the fate of the workshop's chief executive should a client's check not be forthcoming. Once procured, these paychecks are proudly and less than discretely displayed to the surrounding crowd. A few recipients set off for the administrative offices to continue this activity with the authorities more directly responsible for payday.

The entrance to the administrative offices is papered with hundreds of community service announcements. There is also a series of plaques commemorating important patrons of this charitable enterprise. The office area is a cordoned-off section of an otherwise warehousy interior with hollow paneling and partitions thrown up to designate officialdom. The group of recent payees arrive at the secretary's desk and announce their desire to see "Paul," the chief executive of both the workshop and the residential enterprises. Paul, a husky man in his early forties, who sports a crewcut and a disarming smile, emerges from his inner sanctum and assumes a dramatic pose before his secretary: "What is all this commotion? I have business to carry on!" This announcement incites the incipient levity of the group. One man steps forward displaying his paycheck: "I got paid, Paul. I wanted you to see." "I can't believe it. Are you sure?" Paul counters with affectionate sarcasm. "I've been working," says the spokesman and waves the check again. "The cardinal rules," says Paul in an aside to us, "are 'no work/no pay' and 'who's the boss.'" He reminds the group that the workday is not quite over.

Solicited for a number of such paycheck inspections, as we are eagerly welcomed into the sociology at River, we find the contents of these envelopes not only indisputably meagre but also beyond the numerical sophistication of most of the recipients.

THE RICHEST PERSON IN THE WORLD

One such solicitor whom we would get to know better was Frances. Her irrepressible pride in her paycheck was backed up by an equally unabashed display of ignorance regarding its contents. Knowledge seemed irrelevant. Though she had no idea how much she had earned in the previous two weeks and was wholly uninterested in pursuing any calculation of entitlement, she was quite firm on the notion that she had "earned" a paycheck nevertheless. Moreover, it was her impression that everyone in the workshop earned the same amount and that this sameness bore some relation to the sameness of the work performed in the workshop, or as she put it, "Everybody works the same." Asked if she would like to earn more, she said the current pay was enough to satisfy her purchase wants, which consist primarily of additions to her rock-and-roll collection. Asked if she could envision a job that paid more, she could not. Asked what she imagined the richest person in the world does for a living, she replied engagingly, "I am the richest person in the world."

A slight woman who looks somewhat older than her thirty-five years, Frances came to River a few years ago from a large public institution for the mentally retarded where she had spent almost all of her life. She speaks in abrupt phrases, which reflect as much about the vocabulary of the company she grew up with as about her own innate limitations, and she displays the emotional reserve that is the mark of brighter institutionalized people who learned how to fend for themselves at an early age.

Frances has no active family or social relationships outside of River, except perhaps the "boyfriend" she left behind at the institution. Frances is used to living in a confined society, consisting solely of retarded people whose lives are ruled by a wholly separate society of—sometimes benevolent, sometimes not—nonretarded people.

For Frances, the daily work in the River sheltered workshop is simply part of life in an institution glowingly different in character from that in which she spent her preceding thirty years.

The building in which Frances grew up resembles, in its

interior, an antiquated gymnasium. Approximately thirty beds are lined up, side by side, along each of the two far walls, so close together that one must presumably enter his or her bed by climbing over its foot. There are no Monet or Wyeth prints or Scandinavian-inspired wall hangings; the walls are completely bare except for an ancient coat of institutional green paint. The smell is neither Pierre Cardin nor Chanel No. 5 nor even Lysol; it is urine and feces and body odor. In the thirty yards between the two rows of beds, there is nothing, nothing, that is, except people—attendants, most often in groupings of two, and people in ill-matching outfits railing at demons, naked people squatting in silence, people communicating without understanding.

Frances's memories of this institution are not fond. What was it like?

> Didn't like it. You couldn't go out in the summertime; you couldn't have any freedom. Everytime you wanted to go out, there would be quarantine so you couldn't hang around no other building. All you had to go out on was under a tree and that was it.

The restrictiveness of work in River is linked in Frances's life to the relative freedom of life after three o'clock.

It can take Frances almost an hour to traverse the few hundred yards that separate the workshop from her beloved Stott House. As she carefully maneuvers her walker for an even surface, the journey requires constant attention to detail. It is uphill; it is exhausting and downright taxing for so small an accomplishment. But Frances really shines going home, and one reason it takes so long is that she stretches every aspect of the journey, buttonholing passersby for the latest gossip, or simply stopping to admire one of the many sylvan vistas the hill provides. She craves mobility on all planes, from the opportunity to negotiate her own geography to trips that take her to unfamiliar places. She takes immense pride—as she does in her job—in discovering things on her own. She cannot think of a way to improve on the River life, which sent her to Florida last summer, unless it would be more opportunities to "go places."

Standing in Frances's room, one might imagine a college dormitory. The two obligatory twin beds with matching dressers are here. Her stereo puts out rock music, and she has a large record collection. Posters of rock singers spot the walls. In place of the house mother or head resident are house parents, Bill and Laurie, and their baby, Jonathan. No cooks or maids assist. Each of the residents must care for his or her own room and share in the cooking and the cleaning of the common rooms.

Frances has been acquainted with the institution of work since she took her first steps. At the institution, a partial paralysis kept her in a wheelchair for many of her early years, but as soon as a thoughtful social worker discovered her proficiency with a walker, she was assigned a job as a domestic aide. For this job, she was occasionally paid a menial wage, but she was mostly not paid at all, and there was no pattern or rule that she could discern determining when she was paid and when not. Frances understandably thinks of remuneration as more of a gratuitous aspect of work. "Everybody works," she insists.

Frances liked her job as a domestic worker because it afforded her more mobility than was otherwise possible in the highly regulated life of the institution. She would like to do domestic work again, but she has the impression she would have to return to the institution for that privilege, a fate worse than death. Comparatively, River, where "there's a lot going on" and "you can go places," is Utopia, and it is this more transcendent experience of membership in the River community to which she holds the institution of work accountable. Work is simply a fact of life that she subsumes within the more pervasive meaning of River. The River community gives work meaning. Frances was poor in the institution; she is rich at River.

BENCHWORK

The interior of the largest of the workrooms at River workshop has exposed metal beaming, raw concrete walls, and hanging metal lamps. Half-filled cardboard boxes are strewn about among work tables; a disheveled pile of discarded cardboard reaches the ceiling in one corner; there are mounds of industrial widgetry. The largest and most numerous of the boxes display the trademark of a well-known manufacturer of photography equipment, and most of the widgetry looks like film cartridges in various stages of disassembly. This is a large contract for the workshop, and the manufacturer is one of its most prized patrons. Frances describes the arrival of this contractor's shipment like some ceremonial rite, with all work coming to a brief hiatus and the "guys" organized to unload the precious cargo and the "girls" cheering the "guys" on.

Toward the center of the work space, the room resolves into greater organization. Approximately fifty mentally retarded workers are situated at long, elevated tables arranged in parallel, where work tasks have been set out in standardized units. The nature of the work is surprisingly simple (even if one compensates for the clientele), involving one- and two-step assembly and salvage operations. The photography contract consists of separating the unused film from the plastic cartridge and placing the two components in separate boxes. Boredom is not an uncommon complaint among workshop laborers.

Each worker has her or his own individual work quota.

The terms of compensation are piecework rates that bear a sliding-scale relationship to the minimum-wage base and vary with the measured productivity level of each worker. Only a few workers are on the minimum-wage base, which means only that they have an opportunity to work toward the minimum wage. They are known as the *competitive track*, signifying that their rate of productivity is competitive with that range documented in private industries with similar jobs. None of the workers knows exactly what the minimum wage is, and no one earns it, though it is vaguely apprehended that the competitive track is the place to be.

Generally, the better contracts are reserved for the more productive workers, one reason that workers refer to jobs not by task, but by contract name. The photography contract acts as a mild incentive for slower workers to improve, though versions vary among supervisors and workers as to why it is such a plum. Management explains that certain contracts provide a superior rate base because contract awards vary in their terms. Though few—perhaps none— of the workers understand the arithmetic involved, some have figured out that it is possible to work less for more on certain contracts. Others simply catch the enthusiasm by osmosis and enjoy the community spirit of working toward the good contract assignments for its own sake.

More explicit motivational schemes have backfired. An "employee of the week/month" award had to be discontinued when workers complained that it was discriminatory; they felt it should more equitably be passed from worker to worker.

A worker's productivity is officially tabbed once a week and adjusted accordingly. A roving team of supervisors constantly monitors individual progress throughout the day and is empowered to adjust quotas on an interim basis.

Frances, who does benchwork in another building,

stacking cocktail napkins for packaging, refers to this main
base of operations as the "zoo," in reference to the constant
background din of noise (spats, infractions, "acting out"). On
this day, as we enter, the "zoo" is remarkably businesslike,
although two management–worker conflicts are in the process of resolution. In one case, a worker has completely un-
done an assignment he has just completed, reassembling
every film cartridge he had previously disassembled. After
some commotion, it is established that he had run out of
work and did not want it to appear that he was not working.
He does not communicate well, and this conclusion had to be
pieced together by strategic inquiry. Vindicated, he settles
down with an adjusted quota and a knowing glance at some
comrades. In another instance, a young man has just
emerged from a small anteroom, where he has apparently
been sequestered by the staff. He announces somewhat be-
grudgingly that he is now prepared to return to the job to
which he was originally assigned and that he promises to
have a better attitude about it. This obviously painful decision
is greeted with bountiful reinforcement by the supervisors,
who also solicit for him by their excessively demonstrative
behavior a warm welcome from some waiting benchmates.
Frances explains, "They tell you where to work; you don't
have no choice."

NINE TO THREE

The workday at River is officially 9 to 4 for those bench-
workers on the competitive track and 9 to 3 for others. The
day is punctuated by morning and afternoon coffee breaks
and a lunch period at 12:30.

By 3:00 on this day, Frances and I had moved out of the
craftroom area and were settled into an administrative office

for a chat. Closing time is a highly audible event at River as workers walk home or wait to be picked up by special vans or family. At exactly 3:00, Frances politely but firmly suggested that my interview format be suspended: "How many more questions you got? It's time to go home."

More precisely, Frances believes that she is on her own time at 2:45, when benchwork is technically called to a halt: "After you clean up your packages; they make you sit in your seat til three anyway. I hate that sittin' down til three."

On the job, Frances gives the impression of constantly analyzing the boundaries between responsibility and privileges and is among the first to identify any ambiguity between the two. In this regard, there are many other versions of the "3:00 sit-down rule" that she so loathes. Frequently, she feels that she has not been given enough instruction to complete a job assignment; she quickly adds that it is not a question of her needing help, but a question of better management. And it is an imposition because she must remain in her seat while management gets things ironed out.

But the very worst time is when there is no work. These occasions are infrequent but are universally abhorred: "Awhile back—it was in the summertime, there was no [contract] work to be done, but they got us in there anyway. People were goin' out of their minds!" When she is working, Frances doesn't think of herself as confined. "Noise" she finds the most distasteful aspect of her working conditions: "People are always yellin' 'Pipe down,' but you can't tell 'em a thing." Noise is an unfair confinement because one is mandated to sit and work. Noise is not such a problem when one is not sitting.

Frances notes that the no-work problem seems to have upset management as well and understands the correlation between the recent initiation of summer outings and periods of contract slump. She now considers these cherished occasions as an entitlement of working at River, reasoning that people ought not to be made to "sit down" when there is no work. Still, these boundary clashes continue to crop up throughout the workday and throughout the year, corrupting an understanding she thought she had.

MAINTENANCE WORK

Though the parking lot is full on this day, little outdoor activity is noticeable. A lone figure slowly pulls a large plastic trash barrel in my direction. He approaches and says, "Hi. What's your name?" I introduce myself and we shake hands. I ask him his name and he says, "Bob," and extends his hand to shake again.

In his late forties, Bob is the only retarded employee at River who always has the same job. Bob is almost a fixture in the workshop community. For many years, he has performed maintenance work, ranging from trash collection and heavy lifting to light carpentry, gardening, and painting. He works with only modest supervision and usually requires only a brief verbal description of the task to be done.

Bob grew up at home. Not eligible for public schooling, he never learned to read or write, though he is quite capable of acquiring at least a working acquaintance with both arts. In Bob's late teens, his father died. Through his mother's contacts, he procured a job at a local hospital doing basic maintenance work, which he describes as "cleaning floors and moving boxes." When his mother, to whom he was very close, became seriously ill, Bob simply stayed home. He was fired. Shortly afterward, his mother died, and his brother found him a place to live at River in Mountain House. Today, he is one of River's success stories, having graduated to independent living in his own apartment located in the town nearby.

After we shake hands and I remind Bob of our previous acquaintance, he takes me around to see his handwork. He shows me a shed he put up, a doorway he has framed, and the cafeteria he has singlehandedly painted. He emphasizes, "I did all of this alone." Doing carpentry, he is tentative and makes many errors, but he always gets the job done.

Bob speaks with relish and obvious pride about maintenance work. Although he aspires to work in a restaurant in town if he must graduate from River altogether, he indicates that maintenance is the "most important" work a person can do. River, which in the past ran a contract cleaning business, used maintenance work as a reward for appropriate behavior. Further, of the retarded people who achieve independence, which is given ultimate status by the management, quite a few work in maintenance positions.

Bob claims that he takes no breaks during the day, other than lunch, and has never missed a day of work. Asked what he would do if he had all the money he ever needed, Bob says he would just continue his work. And, oh yes, he would get married. Bob cannot think of one adult he knows who does not work.

Bob is paid about forty dollars a week. With his monthly government benefit check, Bob is able to pay rent, utilities, and other expenses, and he has five dollars a week for spending money; he is even able to save for the occasional trips that River organizes. Although he would like to earn more money, Bob isn't sure where or how this would happen; he knows his illiteracy is a barrier to greater job mobility. The highest-paying job he can think of is "maintenance work in a restaurant." He has never heard of the minimum wage. Asked what he would do if he received the same amount of money for staying home, Bob responds, "Just come to work."

Bob goes home to a one-room apartment behind the cin-

ema in the town's small commerical center. It is about two
miles distant. Occasionally, he gets a lift with a staff person.
Normally, he just walks. Sometimes, he joins up with River
residents in the evening for bowling or soccer, but these occasions are infrequent; he might attend a movie alone. He tends
to spend a lot of time in front of the fire station, hoping for a
chat with whoever is around. Other than his supervisor, Bob
cannot recall having a visitor in his home, which he maintains
with meticulous attention. On Saturdays, he works around
the house and yard, fixing, cleaning, and painting. His current project is a bookcase. On Sundays, Bob reports, he
"works . . . pretty much like Saturdays."

Although moving out is given substantial importance by
the management at River, many workers feel great ambivalence about it. In fact, if Bob had a million dollars, he
would move back into one of the residences at River.

WORK AND ITS REWARDS

The fact that the River Association for Retarded Citizens
payday is an occasion of celebration does not mean that people in the sheltered workshop are working for the money in
the ordinary sense. Their living expenses are taken care of in
other ways. If they are not living with families, they are living
in other sheltered residential situations—institutions or halfway houses. Even Bob, the maintenance man, with his little
apartment is dependent on his monthly benefit check for his
basic living expenses. It has been pointed out that many or
most of the clients/employees of the River sheltered workshop are unclear not only about the (admittedly somewhat
complex) basis of their paychecks but even about the check's
absolute amount.

What payday is is a social ritual, a ritual of incorporation.

Receiving a paycheck marks the individual as a member of the River social group, and a member in good standing, one who works for a living: "Everybody works."

We would not argue that in attaching this meaning to work the client/workers of River workshop are different from the rest of us—simply that the nature at this work setting is such as to bring this framing of work activity more clearly into focus than is the usual case.

Chapter 8

PARTICIPATORY
ORGANIZATIONS

People who want to make their work in their own way often
need an organization to do it. The solitary potter we visited
frames her work via her own studio and wants no one else to
share the solitude within which she practices her skill. She
finds selling something of a distraction; she might welcome
an organizational connection that would free her from the
need for selling. Even being let alone to work may take a
supportive organizational structure. To sell, to get supplies,
even to have efforts publicly legitimized may mean working
within an organization.

Except for the solitary potter, all the workers we studied
worked within organizations. In some cases (as in the teacher-controlled school), the organization existed in its basic outlines long before this particular group of people decided to
change it so as to give the workers in a part of the organization more control over their work. In other cases, like that of
the fishermen and the pottery cooperative, organization was

brought into existence by the workers themselves to meet their special needs.

One such need is for resources that are beyond the command of any single individual. The Barnham fishermen, rugged individualists at the workplace in their pitching small boats, and ideologically opposed to collective solutions, nevertheless decided that to assert some control over the price of fish, they had to buy out the existing buyer and reorganize marketing as a cooperative. Now, they have to run the cooperative. The pottery cooperative, now a very groupy affair given to coffee drinking and schmoozing on the job and long talking-it-out policy meetings, came together in the first instance for the very practical reason that no one of the members individually could afford the kiln and the work space that they could muster by pooling their resources. The group that put together the Barton school started with the resource base provided by the municipal school system, but they at once recognized that by a collective management, the school would make it possible not only to use given resources more effectively, but also to mobilize additional ones, as in the case of the volunteer labor of parents.

The organizations also enhance members' work experience by providing a resource in helping to get the "tasks of execution" taken care of. The studio and the fishing co-op assist members with sales and accounting, and the school and NEFCO interface with the community in a way no individual teacher could.

Another reason that people who are particularly committed to their own work may still find it expedient to work within an organization is that the organization can constitute a defense against the outside. The teachers at the Barton school, however committed to teacher control and teacher commitment to teaching, just for this reason needed a principal; they needed someone to deal with parents and with the rest of the school system. The fishermen, having started a cooperative organization to market their fish, found that they could turn the organization to serve as a body to press their interests politically on the issues surrounding fishing regulation.

Finally, organization may help to enrich the work at the individual level within the group. Organization has the potential for colleagueship and community, for building collective identity, for expanding the sense of mastery and control from the level of individual work to the collective, organizational level. This set of themes plays itself out very differently among the various groups.

At one extreme, of course, is the sheltered workshop, where there is neither participation by the workers in policy setting, nor any evident demand for such participation. Decisions by management may be perceived as arbitrary and resented, but the fact that there *is* a management that rules and regulates is central to the creation of a setting that defines as workers people who badly need that piece of social identity.

At the other extreme is the New England Food Cooperative, where collective management of work is central to the meaning of the work itself. Work is a political statement. Democracy in the workplace is as much a part of the output as shipments of cheese and potatoes. Working without machinery is seen as an opportunity to share loads. Skill specialization, as in the case of the woman who knows the most about bookkeeping or of the produce buyer, is recognized as a threat to democracy and total participation, needing to be compensated by job sharing and group participation at meetings.

NEFCO has its problems with all this participation. The loose job roles and nebulous job descriptions that have made it possible to share work communally also seem to make it hard to keep things under control. With everyone in charge of everything, somethings sometimes get done by nobody. The full staff meetings, with everyone involved in talking things out, can be long and frustrating—and unproductive of clear decisions. Looseness of organization turns out not necessarily to mean more democracy; it can also mean a lack of formal checks to the power accruing to those with special information, or a particular interest in getting something to happen.

Nevertheless, for NEFCO, participatory organization is still a central issue, not merely as a means, but as a political goal in its own right. "Why would someone want to go crazy working in a collective warehouse for three years?" unless she or he saw it as part of a program of broader social change, as a first step in a new kind of work institution.

Though the pottery studio came into existence with the rationale of resource sharing, participatory organization has come to take on a dynamic of its own in the life of the studio. It has functions in mobilizing and deciding to solve practical problems: How shall we finance a new kiln? What kind of kiln should it be? Should we rent space?

Organization also helps in building a "group image" for the studio, which can define the studio both to outsiders and to those within. Members find that friends and relatives take them more seriously as studio members than as lone (potentially dilettante) artists. Most of the potters also enjoy being represented as members of a "collective" studio. They feel it makes a statement about their style and stance as craftspersons, and about art itself.

Finally, the organization, with its upfront participatory style, has come to constitute for many of its members a kind of warm psychological atmosphere, a supportive world for creativity. Democratic participation is here less central ideologically than in the case of the New England Food Cooperative, for the group process is treated much more as a matter of particular group choice than it is as a general political statement. Nevertheless, participatory governance turns out to be important in the context of sharing and commitment.

The potters have no manager. They have committees to carry out specific tasks, and they rotate key organizational tasks like bookkeeping. Most often, they operate as a committee of the whole, investigating, exploring, discussing, discussing, discussing. . . .

Democratic governance was an important leading idea in the organization of the Barton Model School. For teachers who are seriously engaged with a professional ideology of autonomy and commitment, the adminstrative bureaucracies of the school system are often perceived as a deadening weight. These teachers began the school within an ideology of educational liberation; it was to be a learning environment for both children and teachers, and teacher control, through participatory governance, was central. In sharp contrast to the usual school organization, the principal was to be selected by the teachers as their agent.

Teachers at Barton, for example, are not handed a curriculum by the central office. Rather, they work on committees themselves to review the available texts and materials, and they choose the ones they think best. Most are active in large meetings that attempt to shape and unify the school's pedagogy and philosophy.

Barton's teachers believe that the school's participatory governance enhances their work experience. At the same time, they acknowledge that the committees take up a great deal of time, and that teachers tire of all that involvement.

The participatory arrangement is also threatened by a new social and economic environment. When it was founded a decade ago, Barton school won central office support for its teacher-governance scheme and for the alternative pedagogy it offered town residents. Those were times of high enroll-ments, optimistic municipal finance, and public interest in open education. With enrollment down, town tax revenues declining, and a decided conservative slant to local public opinion, it's hard to say what will happen to the school.

Of all the worker-created, worker-controlled organiza-tions we had the opportunity to observe, the Barnham fishing cooperative is most limited in its objectives. There is no idea that group organization will deepen and enrich work. There is no ideology of democracy at the workplace. There is no desire to participate for the pleasures of sharing. There is, however, a desire to get a better price for fish, and the desire to get a better price led to the co-op, and the co-op to par-ticipatory management.

A handful of fishermen actually mortgaged their homes over a decade ago to get the co-op off the ground. They organized and bought out a small buyer, spending their capi-tal on some worn-out processing and trucking equipment. They hired the buyer in the hopes of capturing the secrets of dealing with the mysterious Boston and New York fish trade. The buyer stayed long enough to teach them the basics, and their own energies have built the organization from there.

With members wary of any financial dealings, and partic-ularly nervous about giving the manager they have hired any real power, the co-op has become a "lean and mean" organi-zation. As members continuously and diligently review ex-penditures, there is little overspending or excess. Also, with everyone more-or-less skeptical of everyone else, there re-sults a fairly even and extensive distribution of member in-volvement in running the organization. Members rotate re-sponsibilities on the board of directors carefully—almost with a vengeance.

The manager ends up working in a climate that he calls

"negative participation." He is well restrained by the membership, and he respects that restraint, but he would like to see the members take positive as well as negative action. They have been so concerned, for example, about getting the maximum financial returns for their own fish that they have severely undercapitalized the co-op. The members have a consistent track record of rejecting the manager's proposals to build, expand, or invest in the co-op. The co-op bank recently granted the co-op a capital expenditures loan, but only on the contingency that the members contribute a larger share of their returns.

The members established the co-op primarily as a marketing vehicle for their catch. They never intended it to have much of an impact on themselves as individual boat-owners. In fact, many view the co-op as protecting or enhancing their independence in small business.

Despite this and the co-op's "lean and mean" organization, the co-op enriches the members' individual experience of fishing work. The organization takes care of marketing and accounting tasks that the fishermen prefer to stay away from, enabling the fishermen to focus their energies on fishing. More subtly but no less importantly, the co-op adds legitimacy, seriousness, and purpose to fishing work. Younger fishermen view co-op membership as a badge of identification with fishing work as a career. Older fishermen are quick to point out that they belong.

Co-op membership also has a public, expressive dimension. Co-op members are viewed differently, more seriously in town and regional politics than their non-co-op colleagues. Co-op members more often represent fishermen in political matters, and the co-op itself has increasingly strong involvement in politics. The co-op serves, for example, as the organizing vehicle to bus fishermen to public hearings on catch limits and offshore drilling.

Overall, the co-op is an anomaly, an organization in spite of itself and its members. Most of its members prefer solitude to organization, but they find the individual financial rewards of organization compelling.

WORKING ALONE WITHIN A COOPERATIVE GROUP

Even within the framework of a participatory organization, work divides as well as joins.

Among the Barnham fishermen, there is a certain camaraderie in coffee klatching before going to sea, drinking after a long day, gossiping at a co-op meeting, but the overriding tone comes through in the popular phrase: "All cooperation ends at the dock."

Once the fishermen are in their boats, they're on their own. They communicate sporadically on the CB and provide mutual help during emergencies, but they usually go out of their way to be away from other boats. Their preference for lonely work has actually gone so far as to substantially diminish the adoption of a highly promising technique called *pair trawling*, which involves two boats working together.

The teachers trade techniques and classroom management ideas and, like the fishermen, share in the governance of their organization. They have not, however, been able to make much headway with actual collaborative work. One of their founding principles was mutual learning based on peer review, and they have made several honest attempts at it. In practice, however, those strong-minded teachers could not deal with peer review, and the practice was abandoned. In similar fashion, "team teaching" has usually involved less working together than innovative scheduling and sharing of individual preferences and talents. Indeed, it appears that teacher control has worked itself out in the Barton school in such a way as to increase the autonomy of the individual teacher in the classroom to the point where the teachers are somewhat more independent of one another than in the average school.

The potters, also, despite their commitment to mutual learning, have never undertaken group design work. Most agree that it would be exciting to do more group work, but the closest they've come to it has been the construction of the kiln—a difficult, but not a very creative task.

The fact that NEFCO differs from the other three organizations in the extent to which the members work in groups may be traced to the nature of warehouse work. NEFCO members see themselves primarily as political and social activists; working in the warehouse is only a means. NEFCO staff don't take warehouse work as seriously as the members of the other organizations take their work.

For the fishermen and the schoolteachers, worker control through collective organization means mutual defense against outsiders, a defense that should make it possible for each to carry out in his or her own way work thought of primarily as individual. For the potters, collective organization makes a shared environment, but within that environment, the work is set in the most individualistic of traditions, that of the creative artist, and the potters practice in parallel communicative independence.

DIRTY WORK AND DIRTY WORKERS

Collective organization also encounters limitations arising out of the participation, in the work setting, of people who are in one way or another not seen as full members of the decision-making group. These less-than-full members of the group often do work that the full members see as less

interesting and as involving less skill: the tasks that are far-
thest removed from the knowledge tasks that interest members are often carried out by nonmembers of the organizations. While preserving the knowledge tasks for members,
this handling of "dirty work" ultimately poses a threat to the
members' ability to control their organization. In addition,
and perhaps equally important, this strategy compromises
the democratic values that the organizations espouse, values
that are themselves an aspect of the members' job satisfaction.

The distinction between full citizenship in the work and
secondary workers is seen most clearly in the fishing-boat
line between captain and crew, where it is undiluted by any
kind of ideology of democratic participation.

The members of the fishing co-op, all boat owners, do
not make the slightest attempt to bring to their relationships
with their crew any of the elements of participation. Captains
often use military metaphors to describe the organization of
the boat. They are, after all, captains, and they often see
themselves as "tough" and "strict," and they believe this
with good reason, for they contend that the productivity and
safety of the boat depends on their strong leadership.

Crew are seen as transient, almost second-class humans.
They depend on the captain for their income, and in a very
direct way, since their salary is usually determined by a "lay"
system that bases the crew's income on a proportion of the
catch. The proportions vary among boats and crew members
with different levels of ability, but the framework of the for-
mula is constant and has remained basically unchanged at
least since Herman Melville described it in *Moby Dick*.

Crew are seen as dependent and basically untrustwor-
thy, as well. In the "old days," crew members would usually
settle into a long-term relationship with one captain. More
recently, such relationships don't seem to hold up. Captains

see natives of the town as opportunists, bouncing in a fickle way from one boat to another in a continuing attempt to get work on "highliners"—the most productive boats. "They come and go like the weather," a captain complained.

On the other hand, there is a degree of suspicion and disrespect surrounding crew members who remain crew members for long, as there is some sense that crewing is a stepping-stone to becoming a captain. Not to take the step to ownership after some years is a sign of weakness, fear, personal difficulty, tragedy, or the mismanagement of one's income.

"Dirty work" in the school is handled by volunteers, parents who take pride in having an active role in their children's education. The teachers also take pride in the arrangement, believing that extensive parental involvement means good community relations and contributes to their own pedagogy. The level of parent involvement and the school's commitment to it are so great that the school has hired a part-time administrator whose job it is to coordinate volunteers.

Like crew members on the fishing boats, parent volunteers are not members of the governing body of the school. Also like the crew, many aspire to formal work in the field or have stepped down from fuller levels of commitment.

Like crew members, parent volunteers take orders in the course of their normal workdays. Teachers plan, establish direction and organization, and fit parents in for special projects. Parent volunteers work with small groups, develop short-term lessons, play musical instruments, or read to small groups. Like the crew, they thus have their own variety of extensive direct involvement with the "resource."

The Pottery Studio's warm groupiness is somewhat diluted by the presence of several kinds of less-than-total participation. In their long, painful discussions of the strategy for financing the new kiln, the members of the studio had to confront repeatedly—and could never wholly solve—the contradictions of a desire to bring in additional paying members and the sense that these new members could never be wholly a part of the collective group.

The studio has gone about establishing an apprenticeship program to provide interested novice potters with a learning experience. In practice, however, the substance of the "program" leans to support of the potters. Apprentices conveniently take care—as part of their learning—of tasks that don't much interest the potters: maintaining inventory, cleaning the studio, and mixing the clay.

Most awkward of all, ideologically, is the role of second-class citizens in the New England Food Cooperative. Volunteers and part-time workers are the solution to the peaks and valleys in work loads, and while some members of the group feel that it would be better to hire two full-time persons, others like the flood of outside energy. But while part-timers are functionally useful, and while the work they do is not sharply differentiated from that of full-timers, their role in the group is still different. Part-timers cannot take on the same responsibility or develop the specialized skill that full-timers can. After a substantial struggle, part-time workers negotiated representation in the decision-making meetings of the collective work group. But in an organization so centered on direct democracy and consensus, their role is still an anomaly.

What, if anything, is wrong with all this? The work gets done, and both the organization members and the "dirty workers" seem happy with the arrangements. One problem is rhetorical: the hierarchical way of getting the work done contrasts with the espoused democratic values of the organizations. This does not trouble the fishermen, but it does concern some of the teachers and potters. Several of them report unease and a perceived need for extreme politeness in their dealings with volunteers/apprentices. In the school and the studio, also, there has been some discussion of finding ways to formally represent the "dirty workers."

The more serious problems seem to crop up around members' control of their own work, the nature of the work experience, and their control of the organizations. In parceling out *any* aspects of the work, members lose direct control over those parts. In so doing, they sacrifice some control of quality of the product.

"Dirty workers" are immersed in aspects of the work that are crucial to the respective final products. Especially in the way it has developed in all three organizations, the division of labor has often placed "dirty workers" in jobs involving direct service: baiting hooks, student contact in small groups, mixing clay. While perhaps repetitive and mechanical, these are also key "foundation" tasks. If not handled well, they could threaten the rest of the work.

These tasks also place "dirty workers" in a position to monitor crucial information. Working directly with bait, the crew also gets continuing, new data on the overall quality of hooks and lines. School volunteers hear about all sorts of things, aside from their immediate tasks, that might influence the overall classroom approach. Pottery apprentices see the telling underside of the studio: they know which supplies are low and what machines are working. They even have the sort of *comparative* view of all the potters that could help the potters build the sort of learning community to which they aspire.

None of the "dirty workers" seems openly involved in an attempt to wrest governance and control of the organizations from the members. Crew and apprentices (parents seem more serious) do play cat-and-mouse games of "yes, sir" and "uppity subordinate" in the control of the work itself, but generally, they keep the organizations out of their entanglements. Still, there are more subtle, still real, issues of governance and control. Simply because they have special information, the "dirty workers" threaten the members' ability to control: the members can't control their organizations well when they don't have *all* the facts. Though they might *want* to pass on important information, "dirty workers" don't have the perspective to know what is truly important. Nor do they have the incentive, in the way their tasks are defined, to transfer the information.

In sum, the way the organizations handle "dirty work" preserves a particular kind of work experience for the members, but possibly at the expense of the members' ability to fully control their work and their organizations, and at the risk of reduced organizational performance. The practice also compromises the organizations' participatory philosophy and establishes boundaries and blockages for the kind of information transfer that can help keep a small organization viable.

MANAGEMENT WORK

Concentrating on the knowledge tasks of their work, organization members have passed off tasks of organizational management in addition to "dirty work" tasks. It is almost as if they regard management work as itself a kind of "dirty work." The fishermen, teachers, and potters don't much enjoy the work it takes to run their organizations, and they've done a great deal to get it taken care of with minimal involvement by themselves. (This negative view of management work is noteworthy in that it contrasts sharply with many job redesign innovations, which often add management tasks as a way of attempting to enlarge and enrich the work.)

The fishermen hired a manager early in their evolution. They never intended to be involved in selling their own fish in the complex New York and Boston wholesale markets. Nor do they want to do more than the barest minimum of accounting or supervision of the unloading and processing operations—though they absolutely want to keep control over all of these.

The teachers also wanted a principal to help coordinate and organize their committees, and to perform the vital function of interface with the community. They, too, made it abundantly clear that giving up these tasks in no way implied that they would relinquish control of their performance. The potters took a different tack, shunning the designation of a managerial position in favor of attempting to define and rotate management tasks equitably among all the members.

The fishermen/teachers' approach and the potters' approach both have their own problems and strengths. The potters all have a better working knowledge of how the studio functions and have direct access to the important kinds of information that come through the managerial perspective. It all takes a *great* deal of time, however, and occasionally costs the organization: members often make mistakes in their initial efforts to carry out a particular task, and they have difficulties making transitions from one set of tasks to another.

The fishermen and teachers get to spend more time on their work, but they aren't always as informed as they might be on key organizational concerns. Their managers carry out the management tasks competently but also threaten members' ability to control their own organizations.

MANAGERS AND PARTICIPATION

In spite of their commitment to their organization's membership, the managers have some difficulties in making the commitment work. Part of their problem is in experience. Each frequently encounters situations in his work that can be met quickly through his own action, without the members' involvement. The fishing co-op's manager, for example, sometimes can get an exceptional price on fish if he can make a commitment to sell a large quantity involving a total price higher than he is authorized to spend quickly.

Another problem is the spectre of dependence. There is occasional longing in the membership of these participatory organizations for outside authority. The manager of the fishing co-op reports with disgust that some members complain because the co-op does not give them a Thanksgiving turkey, in the way that the profiteering local buyer used to.

At the Barton school, too, there is some sense among teachers of wanting more of the responsibility of management taken from them. They gladly accepted the initiatives undertaken by a more managerial teacher who stood in when the facilitator/principal took a year's leave of absence.

Part of the tension of control between members and managers stems from differing self-interests. The daily work of the manager differs from the work of the members. The manager's work is the organization, not the work itself, and it is in that split that difficulties arise. Spending most of his working hours on the phone with fish buyers in New York and Boston, the fishing co-op's manager has for his day-to-day work a set of tasks that differs from those of the members. His whole career path and future are not in any way like those of the members. He is a manager, they are fishermen, and in that initial difference is the beginning of special interests on each side of the relationship.

While the manager spends his days on the phone, hunched over a desk in the co-op's office building (which is nestled in a clump of pines well out of sight of the harbor), the fishermen are at sea, in their boats. In a different way than the manager's, their days are long and hard, draining much of the energy that they might have to invest in the co-op.

Even if they had the energy to put into the co-op, the fishermen probably would not do much because the co-op's management does not much interest them. They like their work, but the aspects of their work that attract them are not those that involve the co-op. Fishing is outdoors; it is conquest, boats, the hunt, the sea—all in sharp contrast to selling and bookkeeping.

The consequences of the manager–member differences in the co-op crop up around several issues, including simple trust. Though they have hired him and have access to his accounts at all times, the fishermen do not entirely trust the manager. "You've got to have faith," one of them remarked. They are not certain that his wheelings and dealings in the wholesaling business are as sharp as he claims, and their uncertainty is compounded by their lack of understanding of exactly what he does. Their uncertainty is not so much a fear that he is pocketing a little money on the side but a fear that he simply is not working hard enough for them.

The fishermen's uncertainty leads them to action that riles the manager; this, in turn, further upsets the fishermen, etc. One form that this action takes is "little hints." The fishermen ask, "Have you tried this strategy? Have you checked that approach?" These kinds of questions upset the manager, as they imply that he might not be doing his job.

Another kind of action that the fishermen take that upsets the manager is inaction. Pleading ignorance of the whole marketing operation, they conspicuously absent themselves from marketing matters and even, occasionally, from the co-op—until there is a problem. Then, they descend on the co-op with a vengeance, and because they have little information, reasonable discussion is difficult.

Barton school's principal is on a different footing from that of the co-op manager. There was apparently a degree of stigma originally attached to the principalship, for the founders of the school originally intended that the most exciting things would occur in the classrooms. Administration was intended to take a back seat.

The teachers and the parents who founded the school rejected the original proposal for an authoritarian, traditional sort of principal, preferring a colleague-gatekeeper. The principal was to be a "front man" for the school, someone who would explain to the external world what the school was all about while the teachers were left to teach and to make policy decisions about the school.

But the principalship has come to be somewhat more than that. The principal does, in fact, represent the school to visitors, of whom there are a large and continuing number. In so doing, he may have gained a sense of responsibility for the subject of his representation, for he has grown increasingly concerned with matters of quality in the school and has begun to take an increased interest in working with the teachers. At the same time, the teachers have begun increasingly to look at him for some of the same sort of guidance and relief for which the organizers looked to their director.

Although the principal has seemingly participated more in the internal affairs of the school, he has done so in a way that has helped to maintain the collectivity. The principal has been seen, and dealt with, more as a facilitator than an executive. He retains some executive powers, and the nature of his work is different from that of the group members. For him, much more than for the co-op manager, helping the group function as a group is the nature of the job.

NEFCO's manager has taken a stance similar to that of the principal, but he has an easier job of making it work. The warehouse staff are more interested than the teachers in running the organization. In fact, running the organization is the primary interest for many of them.

Despite this more ideally participative arrangement, there is still continuing difficulty with the management work. The manager of NEFCO, like the manager of the fishing co-op, has acquired quite a bit of critical knowledge that gives him implicit authority over the other members. Even with everyone working to keep the information flowing, it is still a struggle.

To summarize, the organizations' handling of managerial work raises continuing problems of organizational control and effectiveness, and it causes interpersonal conflicts between managers and members. Not having a manager at all— like the Pottery Studio—eliminates the conflicts but creates problems of performance and accountability.

The principal's approach of attempting to define his work through, rather than apart from, the teachers seems to minimize some of the problems. The facilitator role, however, has problems of its own, not the least of which is that the members whom it is supposed to serve often want stronger leadership.

Even in NEFCO, there is an inherent conflict between the work of running the organization and the work the organization is created to facilitate. They are different kinds of work, and each draws on the limited energies of the workers. If the problem is addressed by having a specialized manager, the work organization now frames two sets of participants with differing interests: those whose work is management, and those whose work is something else. If, as in NEFCO and the Pottery Studio, everyone attempts to manage, there is ambiguity, a continuing need to spell out who is responsible for what, and a clear sense of overload all around. Most members are too busy to work at their own jobs and run the organization as well.

SUMMARY

To summarize, we observed three trends in the participatory organizations we studied:

1. *Development* of the work experience as highly focused on "knowledge tasks" and individualistic to the point of loneliness.
2. *Evolution* of a set of "second-class citizens" in each of the organizations, who handle the members' "dirty work."
3. *Definition* of management work and organizational maintenance as "dirty work"; conflict between members and the managers they hire; and members' loss of control as a result of their distancing from management.

Based on our small sample, we cannot argue that these trends will affect all participatory organizations. On the other hand, it seems clear that organizations designed to enhance the work experience of their members could fall prey to these problems and tensions. Responding to members' immediate interests in their work, the organizations neglect the time and energy-consuming efforts involved in equalizing participation and ensuring that members are really in control of their own organization.

CONTRIBUTORS

The authors wish to acknowledge the following persons for their contributions to this volume.

PETER LINKOW Assistant professor of human services management at Boston University, where he holds a joint appointment in the schools of Social Work and Management. He was formerly executive director of the Massachusetts Association for Retarded Citizens and has served as a consultant and a trainer to numerous human services organizations. Linkow holds the M.B.A. degree from Harvard Business School as well as graduate degrees in psychology and education.

SHARON MORIEARTY Policy Director for the Massachusetts Association for Retarded Citizens, a private, parent-based organization conducting research and advocacy on behalf of mentally-retarded citizens. She holds the A.B. and M.Ed. degrees from Harvard University.

RUSS TANNER A recent graduate of the Department of Urban Studies and Planning at the Massachusetts Institute of

Technology. He has a long-standing interest in collectives and cooperatives.

JOAN WOFFORD A partner in Leadership and Learning Incorporated, an organizational consulting firm in Lincoln, Massachusetts, that specializes in working with school administrators. She received her B.A. in philosophy from Bryn Mawr and her M.A. in teaching from Yale.

INDEX